AQ

ALSO BY LIZ TRAN

The Karma of Success

AQ

A New Kind of Intelligence for a
World That's Always Changing

Liz Tran

**CROWN
CURRENCY
NEW YORK**

CROWN CURRENCY
An imprint of the Crown Publishing Group
A division of Penguin Random House LLC
1745 Broadway
New York, NY 10019
crownpublishing.com
penguinrandomhouse.com

Library of Congress Cataloging-in-Publication Data
is on file with the publisher.

Hardcover ISBN 979-8-217-08664-1
International edition ISBN 979-8-217-09005-1
Ebook ISBN 979-8-217-08665-8

Editor: Amy Li
Production editor: Natalie Blachere
Text designer: Amani Shakrah
Production: Christopher Andrus
Copy editor: Maureen Clark
Proofreaders: Janet Renard and Miriam Taveras
Indexer: Elise Hess
Publicist: Keely Brewer
Marketer: Tara Gilbride

Manufactured in the United States of America

1st Printing

First Edition

The authorized representative in the EU for product safety and compliance
is Penguin Random House Ireland, Morrison Chambers, 32 Nassau Street,
Dublin D02 YH68, Ireland, https://eu-contact.penguin.ie.

For Taia, of course

AQ

Agility Quotient /ə-ˈji-lə-tē ˈkwō-shənt/ (noun)

1. The ability to handle change, uncertainty, and the unknown

2. A new kind of intelligence for a world that's always changing

Contents

Contents

AQ: Two Letters, Substantial Meaning

The beginning of wisdom is to call
things by their proper name.

—Confucius

"I think you should see a therapist," he said. The *he* was my partner. The time was night. We were stuck in an infinite argument loop because neither of us was willing to bend.

"I *have* seen a therapist," I reminded him. "And I don't need one anymore." For two years, I'd worked on my personal growth with Dr. Mann and achieved tremendous results for my efforts. I'd done my diligence. I'd evolved. What else was there to do?

But he was right, too. Contrary to what I believed, I had not fully evolved; I was *rigid*—and that's a very different thing. I was young then, just a few years into life in New York City, but it doesn't matter if you're young or old or somewhere in between: You can become rigid at any time. It happens when you start believing, as I did, that you've already become the most complete version of yourself.

Daniel Gilbert, a professor at Harvard, calls this "the End of History Illusion." It's a psychological fallacy that people of all ages hold, believing that they've grown so significantly that they've "arrived" at the person they will be for the rest of their lives. While we may think there's more change behind us than in front of us, research shows that this is untrue. We change as much in our sixties and seventies as we do in our twenties, but we don't recognize it because the End of History Illusion is a self-reinforcing cycle.

After all, when you think you're done growing (as I did), then you don't chase new perspectives and experiences (like re-entering therapy). This lack of new exposure means that you indeed stop growing. We've all been there, and chances are there are parts of your life trapped in stasis right now. This book is about breaking free, seeing ourselves as changeable, and regaining the agility we need to be the best and truest version of ourselves.

I shared my therapy anecdote with you not because it is extraordinary, but because it is deeply ordinary. It was a small moment—one of hundreds, maybe thousands, in my life when someone or something beckoned me to change, but I resisted. These forks in the road happen constantly to all of us. Sometimes they are obvious, like the chance to switch jobs or upend a habit. Other times, they appear in miniature— small instances when you could have tried something different, something new, but chose more of the same.

Whenever we resist change, it's not from ignorance or stubbornness, but because of the *status quo bias,* a cognitive preference that holds us in a vise grip, compelling us to keep our lives the same at all costs and maintain the status quo. It exists because we all want to feel safe and secure, so we aim for the tidy and predictable. We take our coffee the same way each morning, put on the style of pants we've worn for years, and cling to old opinions for just as long.

There was certainly a time in humanity when this bias was helpful, but now the world is too dynamic, too unstable, and despite our best efforts, we can't hold it still. Thus, we arrive at the greatest conundrum of being human: We yearn for permanence but find only change. Flights get canceled, hurricanes come ashore, and interest rates double within months. Maybe your company lays off staff or imposes a hiring freeze. Perhaps a family member becomes ill. Surprises happen and disappointments abound. In this world of continual change, we can no longer stay planted. We must learn how to fly.

Stability Is a Myth

I could use data and statistics to show you how turbulent the world has become, but first let's turn to the most compelling evidence of all—your life. Think back on the past couple of years and review the statements below; circle the ones that hold true for you.

- A significant financial expense that I did not anticipate popped up.

- A friend or family member surprised me with their actions.

- I had a major change in my professional life.

- I had a major change in my personal life.

- At either work or home, I encountered a problem I'd never seen before.

- I learned a new skill or technology.

- I saw a development in the news that I could not believe was true.

- I felt uncertain about my job security.

- I thought seriously about quitting or changing my career.

- I felt unsure about what the future looks like for me.

If you circled nearly all of them, you're not alone. Change is no longer the exception but the rule, and it's happening exponentially. The members of Gen Z, the youngest generation in the workforce, will have an average of eighteen jobs across six different careers in their adult lives. Compare this to the baby boomers who often stayed in one job for decades, and with the guarantee of a pension, too. Formerly secure positions like legal assistant, financial analyst, and copywriter have already been replaced by generative AI, and no one's job is immune from extinction. This same instability is true for corporations, too. In 1958, the average

4

lifespan of an S&P 500 company was sixty-one years. Today it's eighteen. Individuals and companies alike must learn how to reinvent themselves.

My profession is to be an expert in change. I work as an executive coach to the CEOs and founders of some of the fastest-growing tech companies in the world. I have witnessed their arc from friends coding in an apartment to leaders helming hundreds of employees and millions in funding. Because their businesses change at warp speed, my clients must level up their own skills at that same pace, and they must do it constantly. Of course, my role involves analyzing spreadsheets and decks and problem-solving to deconstruct acute business challenges, but my most important work is to increase my clients' agility. I articulate how they need to grow, call them out when they're rigid—stuck in a mindset, a bias, or a pattern—and then arm them with the tools they need to change.

Not long ago, it was my turn to learn a lesson in agility. During a coaching session, I sat with my client as we reviewed a project. His PR firm had written a low-quality press release about his company. I immediately started brainstorming ideas to improve the structure and content, work I've done for years as an executive coach. Before I could finish my first sentence, my client interrupted me: "Why don't we just use AI?" He opened his browser, fed the chatbot some information, and in twenty-five seconds had a far better press release than either of us could have written.

I've worked as a leader and an executive in tech and venture capital for more than fifteen years. I consider the knowledge and thinking skills I've acquired to be the bread and butter of why clients work with me. In this instance, the problem was solved in a flash, and none of my hard-won experience was required. I wasn't helpful. I didn't need to be there. This clarified something

I'd begun to suspect and could no longer deny. The world is different now. It no longer matters how smart or experienced you are. In a world where stability is a myth, AQ is the aptitude that matters.

IQ → EQ → AQ

When France began mandatory education for all children in the late 1800s, it required a way to assess the "mental age" of students to properly place them in the right classrooms. Two French psychologists, Alfred Binet and Théodore Simon, leaped at the invitation and created the first-ever practical intelligence test. Since then, the Binet-Simon Intelligence Scale has inspired countless other researchers, including Lewis Terman, who transformed the original framework into the Stanford-Binet Test, the standard IQ assessment in the United States for most of the twentieth century.

Terman believed that high IQ indicated genius, and he sought to prove this with a study he launched in 1921 that tracked 1,528 kids with IQ scores over 135, following them for their entire lives as they grew from children to adults, with the research ending only when they died. Active for more than eighty years, Terman's Genetic Studies of Genius was the longest-running study in the history of psychology. At first, the results proved Terman's belief in the power of IQ. These ultraintelligent children, affectionately dubbed Termites, grew into generally healthy and successful adults who finished college, registered patents, and published papers at far higher rates than their counterparts of average intelligence.

However, as time went on, these differentiators diminished.

The vast majority of Terman's Termites grew into regular people: engineers, typists, lawyers, filing clerks, and police officers. Not a single Termite became a Nobel Prize winner or a world-famous artist. In fact, two future Nobel laureates, Luis Alvarez and William Shockley, were rejected from Terman's study because their IQ scores weren't high enough.

Around the same time that the Genetic Studies of Genius started to yield questionable results, our collective attention turned away from IQ toward EQ, when Peter Salovey and John Mayer coined the term *emotional intelligence* in 1990, and Daniel Goleman popularized it with his 1995 book. Suddenly, emotional skills that could not be measured by an IQ test, like self-awareness, empathy, and self-regulation, were recognized as essential to a successful life. Corporations invested in EQ training, schools pushed for emotional literacy, and new movements like social and emotional learning (SEL) became widespread. In the era of collaboration, globalization, and entrepreneurship, EQ surpassed IQ as the must-have aptitude for an interconnected world.

Let's step back to absorb the full timeline. IQ, the product of Industrialization, emerged in the early twentieth century as a mechanism for ranking, sorting, and placing individuals by aptitude, starting with schoolchildren and expanding to organizations like the military, civil service, and higher education. Ninety years later, the rise of knowledge work ushered in EQ, which was needed for new types of jobs that involved less *doing* and more *stewardship*. Suddenly, success required managing up, managing down, and working well with colleagues across cultures, and EQ enabled this highly interpersonal work.

Now here we are, thirty-five years later, in a culture defined by unprecedented technological advancement, and it's clear that IQ and EQ aren't the end of our story. Our circumstances have dramatically shifted since 1900 and 1990, and while I'm not a futurist, and I don't have a crystal ball, I do know we've been looking in the wrong places, expecting IQ and EQ to be enough for our current reality. What we really need is a new kind of intelligence that directly addresses our ability to handle today's ever-fluctuating challenges and opportunities. We need AQ.

The Agility Quotient

The Austrian philosopher Ludwig Wittgenstein once wrote, "The limits of my language mean the limits of my world." Meanings, ideas, concepts, and qualities cannot exist if we don't have the proper words to describe them. Take the German word *Schadenfreude*, for instance, which describes the pleasure found in another person's misfortune. In Buddhist texts, you find its opposite—the Sanskrit word *mudita*, which means the pleasure found in another person's happiness and well-being. Both words, *Schadenfreude* and *mudita*, are terms used to describe complex feelings that we don't have a precise shorthand for in English.

I never knew that I could experience either emotion until I discovered that terminology. After all, the act of labeling something is what enables it to exist. When a new word becomes a part of the vernacular, it expands our capacity to make sense of the world: Take the pop culture terms like *plant-based*, *binge-watch*, and *selfie* that emerged in this generation, for example.

That is what we're doing with the phrase **AQ,** which I define as **the ability to handle change, uncertainty, and the unknown.** My hope is that this phrase makes its way into our colloquial language and gives this aptitude the focus it deserves. By defining AQ as a stand-alone intelligence, we allow it to take its rightful place alongside IQ and EQ as an important, valid, and observable way of being. More than a hundred years ago, IQ established what it means to be intelligent. Then EQ came along and broadened the meaning. Both were helpful frameworks for the time and context from which they emerged, but now our world in flux demands AQ.

Agility is no longer a talent or a nice-to-have personality trait: It's a nonnegotiable orientation toward life. Just as IQ and EQ previously informed how successful or happy we might become, the Agility Quotient is a new kind of intelligence for a world that's always changing. By naming it, we imbue it with the importance it deserves, and we acknowledge its impact on every facet of our lives.

- **Let's use AQ in our job descriptions** (a fast-paced environment for high-AQ candidates) . . .

- **in our home lives** (I'm raising high-AQ children) . . .

- **and to give direction to our choices** (I'm working on my AQ, so let's try someplace new).

We finally have the right language to describe today's most important ability, and now that we've defined it, we can achieve it.

Total Immersion

It makes sense that this book is about radical change, because I wrote it in a year when my life was radically changing. It was the first year of my daughter's life. At age thirty-eight, I was a new mother who had never even held a baby before. I had to diverge from two decades of adulthood spent doing whatever I pleased to placing her at the center of my universe, while also balancing a busy schedule of coaching, writing, and giving keynote speeches on agility.

My mind returned to Albert Einstein again and again during this time. It is said that whenever he was stuck on some unyielding scientific problem, he'd situate himself in his trusty rocking chair with a small metal ball in each hand. He'd think of his problem as he drifted off, and just as he neared the gates of sleep, his hands would slacken, the balls would clang to the ground, and he'd awaken just in time to recall the solution he'd arrived at in his dreams.

I'm not Einstein, but I came to understand his process during the late nights that come with the care of an infant. Feeding my baby in the still, quiet dark, I inhabited a strange liminal space between waking and sleep where, like Einstein, I experienced no conscious filter to my thoughts. In these moments of nursing my daughter, whole formed sentences appeared in my mind like Times Square billboards. I held her with one arm and typed on my phone with the other, doing my best to wrangle the words before they disappeared into thin air.

My friends and family were surprised to see me writing my second book so soon after having the baby. "Don't you want to wait until she's older?" they asked, watching me coach full-time, breastfeed between meetings, and fit in writing at night after my daughter had gone to bed. I agree that it would've made more sense to wait, but I couldn't. Every day with my new daughter was a total AQ immersion, and I couldn't imagine any situation more suited to writing this book. Now I'm passing that immersion on to you by plunging you into the world of AQ.

This book is designed to be a lived exercise in agility. It's a companion text for anyone who could use some grounding in this unstable world. Perhaps:

- You've been bombarded by change and burned out by change fatigue.

- You want to make a big shift but don't know how to begin.

- Your profession is changing around you, and you wonder what you should do.

- It's been a while since you've learned a new skill.

- You feel left behind by changes in the people around you.

- You experience anger, grief, or disappointment when the unexpected strikes.

- You're unsure of what the future holds for you.

The chapters that follow are divided into three sections: "Who You **Are,**" "What You **Think,**" and "What You **Do.**"

"Part 1: Who You Are" is a deep dive into *you*, codifying your natural assets when it comes to AQ. You'll start with a quiz to determine your AQ Archetype—Astronaut, Firefighter, Neurosurgeon, or Novelist—and you'll learn what that means about your motivations, strengths, and weaknesses. We'll also discuss the Stages of AQ, which define what healthy and unhealthy agility look like. This section of the book is the most vital because it explores the world's most important topic—you.

In "Part 2: What You Think," we'll explore how to shift your mindset to become a more agile person. You'll learn the ABC's of Agility, which are four essential ways to think about your life so that you can face change, uncertainty, and the unknown with ease. Each one of these four tools contributes to your becoming a more grounded, brave, enthusiastic, and resilient version of yourself. You'll practice and apply your new tools through case studies and exercises, and in the process raise your daily thinking to the highest Stage of AQ.

In "Part 3: What You Do," we dive into the particulars of your profession, targeting your actions, behaviors, and strategies to bring AQ into the tactile terrain of work. You'll learn what high-AQ teams and managers look like, what to do in unprecedented situations, and how to grow yourself to prepare for the future. By the end, you'll understand how to build a thriving career, no matter what comes at you.

My job as an executive coach is not done until the client sees real and tangible effects from our coaching work. This book follows the same principle. It is brimming with moments that test and grow your agility, and I hope you'll play along by experimenting with the practices. Of course, they might feel strange or push against the bounds of your comfort zone, but this uneasiness is in service of increasing your AQ. I cannot promise comfort, but I can guarantee growth, and by the final page you'll have everything you need to realize happiness and success in our unstable world. Welcome to AQ.

PART 1

Who You Are

Every now and then
a man's mind is stretched by
a new idea or sensation,
and never shrinks back to
its former dimensions.

—Oliver Wendell Holmes

Demanding and Supportive

Imagine being the chief financial officer of a company that loses $15 with every customer order and burns through $11 million each month. How would you stanch the bleeding of that diminishing bank account? This staggering burden landed on Ravi Gupta's shoulders when he joined Instacart as the CFO in 2015. At his first board meeting, Instacart's lead investor, Mike Moritz, did not mince words. Instacart had to change immediately, or they would soon be out of business. "It was the single worst meeting of my career," Gupta said.

That was just the beginning of many wild swings throughout Gupta's tenure at Instacart. In the year following that meeting, they turned the company around and finally started making money. Then this brief success was reversed when Amazon bought Whole Foods, Instacart's biggest partner, and half their customers disappeared overnight. Through times of fortune and misfortune, Moritz was always there for Instacart, even when few others were, and Gupta labels this particular blend of encouragement "demanding and supportive."

"Most people think of demanding and supportive as opposite ends of a spectrum," Gupta writes. "You can either be tough or you can be nice. But the best leaders don't choose. . . . They push you to new heights and they also have your back." My goal for this part of the book, and in my work as an executive coach, is to embody that balance between demanding and supportive. As you learn the fundamentals of AQ throughout the next chapters, here's what demanding and supportive will look like for you.

Supportive: In chapter 1, you'll take a quiz to determine your AQ Archetype, then learn what it means for your strengths, challenges, and motivations. This work is inherently supportive because the Archetypes help you see the best in yourself. I invite you to adopt a supportive mindset as you explore your inner landscape and celebrate how agile you already are.

Demanding: In chapter 2, you'll learn about the Stages of AQ, which are inherently demanding. The Stages clarify what healthy and unhealthy agility look like, and by studying them we raise a clear bar—pushing ourselves with demanding drive to reach peak AQ.

Demanding and supportive—two opposite sides of a coin that alchemize into agility when combined. Under their influence, you'll accept that there's much for you to learn (*demanding*) but feel confident that you can do it (*supportive*). You'll appreciate yourself deeply (*supportive*), while also holding yourself to a higher standard (*demanding*).

We begin with the fun part—the supportive half of the equation. As you venture forth into the world of the Archetypes, I encourage you to become your own greatest supporter, relishing in your gifts and talents at every possible turn.

CHAPTER 1

The AQ Archetypes

The privilege of a lifetime is
being who you are.

—Joseph Campbell

I wonder how long I could last on my own in the Sonoran Desert. It's a harsh expanse of land stretching from Arizona down to Mexico, where the temperatures climb as high as 120 degrees Fahrenheit, and it rains as little as three inches a year. Thousands of migrants, hikers, and adventurers have died while traversing it. What would I do to survive there?

Going off how I typically handle the unknown, I'd throw

myself into research and planning. I would obsessively read all I could about the Sonoran Desert—its flora, fauna, and climate—and write down every worst-case scenario I could imagine. Next, I'd work my way through online forums about desert camping and use this information to pack the perfect gear.

Ninety-nine percent of my preparation for this trip would happen alone, in my mind, far in advance. That's because my AQ Archetype is the *Novelist*. I handle change, uncertainty, and the unknown through proactive planning, and while I excel at preparation, I don't do well with life's curveballs. I am most comfortable with a premeditated, structured path. Like a novelist who sits at their desk building worlds, I thrive when I have the freedom to design my own future.

Alongside the Novelist, there are three other AQ Archetypes: the *Astronaut*, the *Firefighter*, and the *Neurosurgeon*. They have their own quirks and qualities that allow them to be agile. Novelists like me make plans. Astronauts inspire. Firefighters improvise beautifully, and no matter what, Neurosurgeons never give up.

One is not better than the others. Irrespective of your AQ Archetype, you are capable of thriving in the proverbial Sonoran Desert of life, but the first step is to know what Archetype you are at your core. Are you an Astronaut, a Firefighter, a Neurosurgeon, or a Novelist? What skills do you have at your disposal for handling stress, solving problems, and tackling crises? You'll find out when you take the personality assessment in this chapter.

This quiz is a mini version of the in-depth assessment that I use with corporate teams to identify their Archetypes, Stages, strengths, and challenges. Both the full assessment and this abridged version were developed from my work interviewing and observing hundreds of founders and executives.

I'm certified to administer and evaluate four personality assessments and have worked with more than a dozen throughout my career, like the Myers-Briggs Type Indicator (MBTI), Hogan, CliftonStrengths, DiSC, and the Enneagram. What I've learned is that we humans are notoriously bad at seeing ourselves. We undervalue our strengths, imagining that what comes easily for us is not particularly special, and at the same time we can't always see what we lack. Personality assessments give us the ability to perceive ourselves clearly, and as an executive coach, I know that there's no power more potent than that.

Before we jump into the quiz, we need to identify two types of change that occur in our day-to-day: *Proactive Change* and *Reactive Change*. The distinction between the two gives us context for understanding the Archetypes.

Proactive Change is the change we initiate ourselves, like upgrading our homes, switching jobs, or deciding to eat healthier. It's the change we invite into our lives. This change is often considered to be positive and productive, even if it's not always enjoyable. On the other hand, Reactive Change describes how we handle unwanted and unpredictable events, like flight cancellations, illness, or geopolitical conflict. Because it feels jarring and disruptive, this type of change is generally seen as more negative. For every person in the world, life is a succession of Proactive and Reactive Changes, and each Archetype has either a fast reaction or a slow reaction to it.

Figure 1: Archetype Change Styles

	Neurosurgeon	Novelist	Firefighter	Astronaut
Proactive Change	Slow	Fast	Slow	Fast
Reactive Change	Slow	Slow	Fast	Fast

Figure 1. Agility comes from understanding your Archetype's slow and fast reactions and knowing how to make the most of them. Each Archetype, regardless of speed, can achieve high AQ.

We'll delve into these distinctions later, so there's no need to memorize this chart. I simply want to emphasize that when it comes to agility, there's no "best" or "worst" Archetype. It doesn't matter whether yours is slow or fast or some combination. AQ emerges from developing self-awareness about your type and then making the most of your gifts and abilities.

AQ Archetypes Quiz

For each of the following questions, circle the selection that feels most like you.

1. **Which statement best describes your daily routine?**

   A. I know what habits work for me and I stick to them.

   B. I regularly try out new habits. I'm always improving what works for me.

    C. My routine changes based on my top priorities for the day.

    D. I go with the flow of each day.

2. Which is the worst work environment for you?

    A. The culture is chaotic with unclear goals that are always shifting.

    B. My ideas and perspective aren't needed or appreciated.

    C. I don't have the agency or ability to make a real impact.

    D. There is no creativity, imagination, or innovation.

3. What do you optimize for when planning a vacation or holiday?

    A. I prefer plenty of time for research and planning, so I can book in advance.

    B. I'll make a plan, but I need the freedom to change my mind or itinerary.

    C. I don't like too long of a vacation. Just a few days is all I need to recharge.

    D. I always make time for new places and/or experiences.

4. Which work situation would make you the happiest?

    A. Work is stable and steady, and I have everything I need.

B. I have lots of space and freedom in my schedule.

C. I am effective, productive, and doing important work.

D. I have the time to dream up and explore new ideas.

5. How do you feel about routines and processes?

A. I love my routines and processes. They make life so much easier.

B. I like variability but get overwhelmed when unexpected change pops up.

C. I may have a routine, but my day is always flexible.

D. I like routines, but I much prefer new and different experiences.

6. Who do you value most in personal relationships?

A. People who have known me for a long time.

B. People who give me the space to be me.

C. People who I can depend on.

D. People who broaden my world.

7. How do you approach long-term planning and setting goals?

A. My goals are carefully planned and researched with much diligence.

B. I set ambitious goals and reserve the right to amend them.

  C. Sticking to ambitious goals ensures that I accomplish what I want.

  D. I have loose goals but a clear idea of the future that I'm always working toward.

8. **What are you most likely to do in a crisis situation?**

  A. Put in hard work to keep the original plan moving forward.

  B. Feel overwhelmed at first, then explore ways out of the situation.

  C. Jump into action right away and solve the crisis.

  D. Stay positive and look for the silver linings and upsides.

9. **How do you feel about taking risks in pursuit of your goals?**

  A. I will take calculated risks if there is a solid plan in place.

  B. I will take a risk if it creates more autonomy or independence for me.

  C. I take risks when I have the capacity to deal with the outcome.

  D. Risks are essential to innovation and progress.

10. **How do you initially feel when faced with unexpected change?**

  A. Worried: How can I fix this situation?

  B. Annoyed: This wasn't part of my plan!

C. Calm: What's the difference? Life is always in flux anyway.

D. Accepting: This isn't what I wanted, but I can make it work.

11. Which of the following sayings best describes your perspective of life?

A. Build your castle, brick by brick.

B. Life is short; forge your own path.

C. I can do anything I put my mind to.

D. Imagination is more important than knowledge.

Now tally up your answers and determine which letter (*a, b, c,* or *d*) you selected most frequently. Your predominant letter corresponds to your AQ Archetype.

If *A* was your most frequent answer, your Archetype is the Neurosurgeon.

If *B* was your most frequent answer, your Archetype is the Novelist.

If *C* was your most frequent answer, your Archetype is the Firefighter.

If *D* was your most frequent answer, your Archetype is the Astronaut.

If the score between two Archetypes is close, read the descriptions of both and choose the one that resonates most with you. If you still find yourself equally attached to multiple Archetypes after digesting their details, congratulations—you are a blend, and that's completely normal. After all, none of us are caricatures. We're complex, complicated, and often contradictory.

Perhaps your dual identity is rooted in context. Maybe you

show up in one realm of life as a certain Archetype, and in a different realm as another. I scored a whopping 7 points on the quiz as the Novelist, and while it's the Archetype that rings most true for me overall, I am definitively an Astronaut in my professional life, handling Reactive Change with an ease that eludes me in my personal life. Sometimes, when I'm with my family of origin, I even feel like the Neurosurgeon—diligent, detailed, and less comfortable with both types of change.

Do you feel caught between two or more Archetypes? Ask yourself whether you connect with one Archetype over another in certain domains of your life. Or do specific communities, environments, or groups of people bring out one Archetype within you? The most common split for people is who they are at work versus who they are at home, but various situations can incite different Archetypes.

Time can also be a factor in our expression of the Agility Quotient. Perhaps you were a Novelist in your younger years but adulthood brings out your Neurosurgeon tendencies. Some notable personality inventories maintain that your type cannot change. The Myers-Briggs Type Inventory says that if you're an extraverted, intuitive, feeling, judging type (ENFJ), you'll be one for life, and the same is true for the Enneagram, which contends that essential personality can never be altered. The AQ Archetypes are innately different because they're founded on the premise that we can and should change. I know this is true, because I've seen it happen time and time again with clients.

Take, for instance, one client I've worked with for five years. When we first met, she was a Firefighter through and through, which is the perfect Archetype for extinguishing the many fires early-stage startups face. As her company grew a thousandfold into new products and geographies, she pushed herself to be more planful and fine-tune her skill of foresight. In the process, she mastered Proactive Change and transformed from a Firefighter to an Astronaut.

Even if you don't change your Archetype completely, you may find that you absorb the talents and tools of the other Archetypes as you increase your AQ. Perhaps you flex into the Neurosurgeon when excellence is needed, or you adopt the mindset of the Astronaut when it's time to dream big.

While you may see two or more Archetypes in yourself, there will always be just one that serves as your dominant approach. You can think of it as your average, your default, your factory settings. There will be many more opportunities in this book to explore the Archetypes in depth, so feel free to investigate just your dominant one, or work with all the Archetypes you see in yourself. Let's get started.

Archetype #1: The Neurosurgeon

Slow at Proactive Change
Slow at Reactive Change
Motivated by Excellence

The Neurosurgeon is focused. She's on her feet for a twelve-hour surgery that demands her full concentration. Her operating canvas is merely millimeters wide, and if she slips by even a fraction of a millimeter, her patient may die or become permanently disabled. The Neurosurgeon is equipped for this high-intensity work because of her diligent preparation. She's spent more than fifteen years studying medicine, and she operates at a standard of excellence that the other Archetypes may never experience. The

Neurosurgeon embodies this fundamental truth: **The greatest things in life take time.** She is proof that slow and steady wins the race.

We might not look at the Neurosurgeon and immediately think of agility; after all, this type is slow at both Proactive and Reactive Change, but Neurosurgeons are agile in their own way. It may take them longer than most types to respond to new events and information, but once they've set their mind to something, they won't stop until they've achieved it. **Neurosurgeons are determined, resilient, and motivated by excellence.**

Take Nicole, for example, a conference producer in her forties who manages tight budgets and huge crews of people to bring her projects to life. Her colleagues see her as exacting and persistent, diligently steering a project over many months or even years. She knows how to take her time. "We can't just jump from A to Z," she says. "First, we must go from A to B, then C. If we go too fast, everything will break, and we'll be right back at A again." Nicole is a perfectionist who believes that there is a right way to do things.

In her personal life, Nicole is equally steady. She's still close to her childhood friends, and she makes a great effort to maintain and invest in those oldest relationships. When she graduated from college, she moved into a modest apartment and then she stayed there for ten years, even as her income grew and she could afford a nicer place. When Nicole ultimately decided to buy her own home, it took four years of rigorous house hunting before she put in an offer. As you can see, Proactive Change happens slowly for Nicole. Before making a big leap, she must research and learn until she's achieved a high level of expertise.

When it comes to Reactive Change, Nicole also goes at her own pace. As a Neurosurgeon, she must step back, assess, and process the shifts that are happening to her, unlike some of the other Archetypes who leap into action. Reactive Change feels deeply stressful to the Neurosurgeon, and it may even take years for Nicole to make peace with the new reality and find a path forward.

Fast pivots, big risks, and constant reinvention are not the Neurosurgeon's wheelhouse. Still, Neurosurgeons can be impressively agile in their own way. They make the impossible happen, not through sleight of hand, but through intense dedication and resilience. They become experts in whatever they put their mind to, and they never quit until their goals are completed. We need high-AQ Neurosurgeons to produce the meaningful, structural change that our world so desperately needs today, because **Neurosurgeons move mountains, boulder by boulder.**

The Neurosurgeon at a Glance

The Neurosurgeon is motivated by excellence: The Neurosurgeon holds every aspect of their life to the highest of standards, moving with diligence, conscientiousness, and hard-won expertise.

Strengths: The Neurosurgeon is steadfast and determined, and once they commit to something, they never give up until they've succeeded. Neurosurgeons are also a steady and stabilizing force for everyone in their lives, and a source of incredible expertise and wisdom at work.

Challenges: The Neurosurgeon's perfectionism can become a fear of failure. They see the world with more skepticism than optimism, and this leads to them saying no to change more than they say yes. They are slow in times of turmoil.

Antidote: The Neurosurgeon must learn to befriend discomfort. They grow by forcing action and decisions at a faster pace than what is typical for them, extending the boundaries of their comfort zone.

Archetype #2: The Novelist

Fast at Proactive Change
Slow at Reactive Change
Motivated by Freedom

As the Novelist embarks on his work of writing, he sits alone, dreaming up people and places that don't exist. He plans. He lays down a timeline, a plot, a structured path for his hero to follow. **The Novelist is the master of mapping out change.** He knows exactly how to bring his vision to life and has designed all the steps in between.

But then the Novelist's phone rings. It's his editor calling with an urgent question. This jolts him away from his work, and he's annoyed. Then he hears the smoke alarm beeping—low batteries need to be changed. On the way back to his desk, he checks his phone. There's an email from his kid's school, a past-due bill to be paid, and an avalanche of texts that need a response. Finally, the Novelist gets back to his computer, only to find that the dog has chewed through the charger cord. He is flustered, frustrated, overwhelmed. The unexpected chaos of life has prevented him from actualizing his plot, and he detests it. Why can't things just go the way he wants them to?

The Novelist's agility stems from his profound gift for envisioning the future. He can glimpse possibilities that others can't discern. He creates a detailed world in his mind, then takes bold steps to make it real. **The Novelist is the most skillful Archetype when it comes to generating Proactive Change,** pivoting and pushing to transform his intentions into reality. The change he didn't ask for is harder to stomach, though. He can't stand it when he's not the one writing the story.

In my post-college professional life, I have been a legal assistant, an LSAT teacher, a waitress, a recruiter, an HR director, a consultant to Fortune 500 companies, a yoga and meditation teacher, a venture capital executive, a podcast host, a leadership coach to CEOs and founders, a keynote speaker, an author, and now a founder myself. Like a writer with his main character, I have constantly remade myself. I am comfortable forging new friendships and connections and entering unknown worlds. I am fast at Proactive Change, and I'm at my best when I'm working toward an audacious goal. It's how I express control over my life.

Novelists like me have the opposite experience when it comes to Reactive Change that they haven't asked for or planned for. I am thrown off track when a flight is canceled. I collapse when the plans I've hashed out suddenly veer off course. I struggle with the regular wrenches and disappointments that make up daily life. **Novelists thrive when it comes to the changes they've chosen but struggle when they don't get a say.** Like the Neurosurgeon, the Novelist may freeze in moments of Reactive Change, and they need weeks, sometimes years, to accept the new normal.

If you are a Novelist, remember that your mind is a powerful tool. You are able to envision a bold, new future for yourself with detail and clarity. Then, like the scribe at his desk, you work steadily until it becomes real. Novelists play an important role in this world—they dream. They don't accept that life must be as it is; they see a better way and then they use their agility to generate a new story. **Novelists move the plot forward. They push for change. They reinvent themselves and the world around them.**

The Novelist at a Glance

The Novelist is motivated by freedom: The Novelist is unafraid to deviate from the past; thus, they thrive in situations where they are allowed to change directions whenever they want. The Novelist is motivated by freedom—they demand the agency to write their own story.

Strengths: The future-forward Novelist is at the leading edge of their field and up-to-date on the latest news. There's always a bold goal, a big insight, or an exciting book to discuss. Their enthusiasm for Proactive Change is inspiring to those around them.

Challenges: The Novelist uses change as a way to avoid difficult situations. In hard times, they'd rather pivot than persevere to the finish. Also, when unwanted change rocks the Novelist's world, they can become overwhelmed and lash out.

Antidote: The Novelist only grows once they learn

how to let go of their plans and expectations. When Reactive Change happens, they must work hard to fight their natural inclinations and embrace reality. Peace comes for the Novelist once they can see the silver lining in unwanted change.

Archetype #3: The Firefighter

Slow at Proactive Change
Fast at Reactive Change
Motivated by Impact

Quick! Every second counts. There's a fire on the second floor, a family trapped on the third, and less than a minute to decide what to do. The smoke is thick and the roar loud, so taking stock of the situation is impossible. Luckily, the Firefighter has arrived. He's fast. He sprints to the scene, hurls directions to his team, and rushes in to save the day. He comes alive in circumstances that would leave others frozen in fear. He has stores of energy, an upbeat attitude, and a calm disposition.

The Firefighter chooses this dangerous line of work because he knows that he can make an important impact amid chaotic situations, and he plays this role in his personal life, too. **He's the crisis hotline for his loved ones. He's the one you ring when you don't know who to call. He solves unsolvable problems. The Firefighter doesn't understand the meaning of** *can't.*

Firefighting isn't just about handling catastrophic events. The Firefighters among us deftly manage challenges and daily disruptions, too. Take Florian, who runs a successful chain of cafés, for instance. In his work, hiccups occur on a daily basis, from a broken heating system to a hornet infestation, to suppliers who show up with the wrong inventory. Now multiply those issues by thirty locations, and add in the stress of responsibility for a hundred employees. Florian's day often goes off the rails, with unexpected emergencies usurping his planned meetings, but he doesn't mind. In fact, he thrives in chaos. **The wilder a situation gets, the calmer and more focused the Firefighter becomes.**

Notice how Firefighters like Florian and Novelists like me are opposites. Even just imagining myself immersed in the spontaneous, unplannable nature of Florian's work makes me feel anxious. I know that I would freeze up and panic in his job. This is because Novelists struggle to deal with the Reactive Change that Firefighters easily manage. Conversely, Firefighters often struggle to prioritize Proactive Change, which is the Novelist's specialty. Firefighters are so skilled at in-the-moment responses that they can often neglect planful, future-oriented endeavors. They figure, *Everything changes anyway, so why waste time with plans that won't stick?*

Not long ago, I was walking with a group of friends after taking in a Broadway show together. Times Square was teeming with people, and dozens of strangers flowed past us every minute, including an older woman with a cane. Just as she walked in front of us, she tripped on a divot in the sidewalk and fell to the ground with a loud cry. Among the throng of countless passersby, no one moved to assist her. The whole crowd was frozen, unsure of what to do, except for my friend Lauren, who jumped in immediately to help the fallen woman. Lauren doesn't have a high-octane, high-risk job. She is an architect and would never choose to work as an actual firefighter, yet she embodies the

Archetype to a tee. When there's confusion or conflict, she leaps to fix it, bringing harmony and calm to high-intensity situations. Firefighters are rarely showy or brash. Their level heads and tranquil demeanors mean they often fly under the radar, but if you pay attention, you'll start to notice them everywhere.

The colleague who steps in to save the day, the family member who takes charge in an emergency, the stranger who rushes to help you with your stroller—I hate to imagine a world without Firefighters. We'd all be trampling one another, beset and harried. The fact is, there are more emergencies than we've ever seen before. Droughts, wildfires, data breaches, stock market dives, Web outages, and layoffs are commonplace now, and we need our coolheaded and ingenious Firefighters more than ever. **They bring calm when there is chaos. They solve problems that appear impossible. They are who we need in this surprising and ever-shifting world.**

The Firefighter at a Glance

The Firefighter is motivated by impact: The Firefighter is an expert at fixing what others believe to be unfixable. Doing work that really matters is a necessity, and they thrive on seeing the tangible results of their efforts.

Strengths: The Firefighter excels when most people would feel stressed out, anxious, or paralyzed. They have huge stores of energy, an upbeat attitude, and a calm demeanor. The Firefighter sees possibility in impossible situations. They aren't deterred by setbacks and surprises. In fact, these shocks keep the Firefighter's mind sharp and alert.

Challenges: All the time spent fighting fires leaves very little room for the Firefighter to be intentional and strategic about the future. Because they do well in emergencies, the Firefighter can tolerate high levels of stress, and sometimes may create chaotic situations, because that's where they feel comfortable.

Antidote: The Firefighter must push themself to become as adept with Proactive Change as they are with unwanted change, making the time on a quarterly or annual basis to draw up big-picture plans.

Archetype #4: The Astronaut

Fast at Proactive Change
Fast at Reactive Change
Motivated by Passion

Mae Jemison set off into space in 1992, accompanied by her Alpha Kappa Alpha sorority banner, a statue from a West African women's society, and an army of female frogs to fertilize and study. In NASA's entire history, only 360 individuals have been selected as astronauts, and when you read through Jemison's biography (Stanford, Cornell, Peace Corps), it seems obvious that she would become one of them. At the time, however, it was anything but a given. Mae Jemison was the first African American woman to travel into space, and not only did she have to stand out from thousands of other qualified candidates, but she also had to break down barriers of racism and sexism. Looking back on her career, Jemison famously said, "Never be limited by other people's limited imaginations."

Never be limited by other people's limited imaginations. Mae Jemison's words are the perfect slogan for the trailblazing Astronaut Archetype, who is forever pushing toward new horizons. Picture an astronaut on a space walk—floating free, buoyant and weightless, with nothing but a slim tether connecting her to her known world. The Astronaut does not mind. After all, she's used to doing things her own way. **When it comes to agility, the Astronaut is characterized by individuality, authenticity, and passion.** The Astronaut doesn't follow trends. She doesn't copy what everyone else is doing. Instead, she is uniquely herself, with singular interests, and ready to bound off wherever this curiosity takes her.

Anna is an Astronaut Archetype, and she is working on something that has never existed before. She is the founder and CEO of a biotech company, and she spends her days with stem cells and bioreactors, hoping to change the future. She is passionate about her work and driven by purpose, but when she explains her mission to others, it sounds like science fiction. None of this matters to Anna, because her dreams are so clear. **That's what Astronauts do—they pursue singular paths others may not understand.**

Anna's sister, Emma, doesn't work in science, but she's an Astronaut, too. She dresses in bright, bold clothing that others regard as audacious, but in her eyes she's just being herself. Emma was a social worker, then a legal assistant, and now she works in publishing. Her career may seem haphazard and nonlinear, but she knows what interests her and she follows that passion; so far, it hasn't led her astray.

Astronauts, no matter their industries or interests, have incredible powers of foresight, but this gift can feel frustrating. After all, few people can keep up with the Astronaut's pace of ideation, so they often face skepticism, misunderstanding, and doubt from those around them. To become their most agile, Astronauts, ironically, must learn to slow down when it comes to both Proactive and Reactive Change, and to get good at explaining their perspective, step-by-step, to others. They must learn how to translate their audacious insight into digestible plans.

When they can do this, Astronauts become the most inspirational of the Archetypes. They spark hope and enthusiasm. They catalyze revolutions and movements. Astronauts energize the collective, and we need them more than ever today. The world's rate of change has become exponential; thus, our thinking must grow exponentially, too. Without the Astronaut we'd be stuck—stuck in what we know, stuck in the status quo, and as Jemison said, *confined by the limits of our own limited imaginations.* Luckily, the Astronaut beckons us on an adventure.

The Astronaut at a Glance

The Astronaut is motivated by passion: Astronauts follow their passion, whether personal or professional. Their vivid interests and curiosities inform every action and decision. Their intense enthusiasm drowns out any fear, so they hardly register big shifts that can unravel other people.

Strengths: The Astronaut is fast. They are quick to evolve and pivot, moving more swiftly than the other Archetypes. Another gift is authenticity. They are unapologetically themselves, with a unique approach to their life. This combination of speed and passion creates a bold and decisive personality.

Challenges: The Astronaut can be so absorbed in their passion that they overlook the boring and tedious details needed to embark on their grand adventure. They may feel like they're making great strides mentally—envisioning the big picture—but that progress isn't always reflected in the real world. The Astronaut's goals may stall from poor follow-through or difficulty rallying others behind their vision.

Antidote: In order to make the most of their natural agility, the Astronaut must learn how to slow down to translate their bold aspirations into digestible and logical components. To find success, they must buckle down to complete the tasks and responsibilities that aren't their passion but are still necessary.

Now we've arrived, having completed our tour through four different worlds. After exploring your Archetype, I hope you feel proud of who you are and the unique agility skills you possess. Even if there were parts of your Archetype's description that didn't feel 100 percent like you, don't dwell on them. The purpose of this exercise is not to match your paradigm perfectly but to give you a thematic lens for self-observation. I doubt anyone will read their Archetype and agree with every descriptor. But that's a good thing, because the Archetypes were intended to be maps, not photorealistic portraits, and like the best maps, they allow for many possible routes. The primary goal of this chapter was to spend time appreciating *you*. Now let's take a moment to appreciate the people you know, too.

Figure 2: AQ Archetype Summary

	Motivator	Strength	Challenge	Life Motto
Neurosurgeon	Excellence	Determination	Slowness	Build your castle, brick by brick.
Novelist	Freedom	Vision	Overwhelm	Life is short; forge your own path.
Firefighter	Impact	Steadiness	Chaos	I can do anything I put my mind to.
Astronaut	Passion	Speed	Impatience	Imagination is more important than knowledge.

Figure 2. The Archetypes support, complement, and inspire one another.

Agility Advisors

People often ask me if like attracts like when it comes to the Archetypes. Do Astronauts go with other Astronauts, and should they avoid Firefighters altogether? Do Neurosurgeons and Novelists, so different in temperament, annoy each other? The answer is both yes and no. Most of the time, the Archetypes do not get along with one another. Astronauts think Neurosurgeons don't understand them, and Firefighters' spontaneity annoys Neurosurgeons. Novelists think that Astronauts could be more organized, while Firefighters just want everyone to calm down. I could go on and on about how the Archetypes frustrate one another, but the point is, when we operate at our default settings, we find people who are unlike us to be the most challenging.

However, agility changes all this. Once you understand what makes the other Archetypes tick and the unique assets they offer, your aversion wanes and your appreciation grows. My own example of this is my twenty-year friendship with three college friends. I am a Novelist, and each of my friends is a different type. When I shared the Archetypes concept with them, it deepened our connection. Now we can see that we are objectively better together, because we learn from one another, augment one another's weaknesses, and can divide and conquer big tasks.

Here's an easy and effective suggestion as you kick off this new AQ journey: Hang out with the other Archetypes, especially the ones who see the world most differently from you. Let your personal mission be to find **Agility Advisors**—friends, family members, and colleagues from each of the four Archetypes— whom you can call upon when you might benefit from their insight. With a diverse cast of Agility Advisors in your life, you can solve any problem, no matter how unfamiliar it is to you.

For instance, if you have a big decision to make and you can't afford a mistake, call the **Neurosurgeon**. Their thorough thinking will force you to investigate every nook and cranny of possibility. What if you're stuck in a rut and don't know how to get out? I'd suggest you contact a **Novelist**. They'll imbue you with the proactive courage you need to take a big leap and help you develop a plan to make it happen. Of course, in a crisis, you'll want to consult your **Firefighter** friends. The more flustered you are the calmer they'll be, ready with quick action in emergency situations. Finally, you also need an **Astronaut** in your life. After a big disappointment or defeat, they will buoy you up. If you're doubting yourself, they will remind you to trust yourself, live authentically, and take a leap into the unknown.

When it comes to agility, we shouldn't have to go it alone. In the office and at home, make it a game to find out the Archetypes of the people around you, then don't be shy about asking for their input. Pepper them with questions. Step into their shoes. It doesn't matter whether you take their advice or not. The simple practice of seeing through another's eyes is in itself an act of agility.

With this exploration of the Archetypes, you've initiated your journey into the world of AQ. Next, we will shift into the *demanding* side of the "demanding and supportive mindset" as we turn to the **Stages of AQ** to assess how agile we really are. Are you ready to see how you measure up?

Archetypes Exercise

Bring to mind a big moment of change, whether Proactive or Reactive, and consider how your Archetype influenced your response.

For example, as a Novelist, I researched and made a comprehensive plan for sleep training my infant daughter. In the moment, however, I got overwhelmed when my baby wouldn't stop crying. I had to lean on my husband, a Firefighter, to decide our next steps, because he thrives in high-pressure situations.

CHAPTER 2

Everything Changes

Nothing is absolute.
Everything changes,
everything moves,
everything revolves,
everything flies
and goes away.

—Frida Kahlo

In 1968, outside of Big Sur, California, a Zen teacher named Shunryu Suzuki spoke on the nature of Buddhism to a rapt audience. One student, David Chadwick, was enthusiastic but confused. "Suzuki-roshi," he said, "I've been listening to your lectures for years, and I really love them . . . but I must admit I just don't understand. . . . Could you just please put it in a nutshell? Can you reduce Buddhism to one phrase?"

The whole room laughed at the student's preposterous desire to distill a 2,500-year-old philosophy into a handful of words, but the teacher was calm and unfazed. Suzuki turned to the confused student and responded with just two words. "Everything changes," he said, and moved on to the next question.

Everything changes. It's as simple as that. It was true at the beginning of our human existence, and it is true now. And it's not just *change;* it's also *uncertainty,* and the *unknown*—the unyielding vagaries of life that disrupt our happy status quo.

CHURN

Throughout this book, we'll refer to these ebbs and flows of living as *CHURN,* which stands for *Change, Hiccups, Uncertainty, Rupture,* and *Newness*—essentially anything that disrupts the status quo. *Change* means a shift from one state to another. *Hiccups* are the small obstacles that veer us off course. *Uncertainty* is when we don't know what the future holds, and *Rupture* is a sudden, surprising occurrence. Finally, we experience *Newness* whenever we embark on unfamiliar experiences. When we talk about CHURN, we mean the things that knock us around, those uncontrollable waves, big and small.

Let's consider CHURN through the lens of an ordinary trip to the grocery store. Imagine that you've just arrived when your partner calls you with a few items they forgot to add to the shopping list (a *Change*). At the market, you can't find the main ingredient for tonight's dinner (a *Hiccup*), and you're not sure what to do (*Uncertainty*). While bumbling around the store, you accidentally delete your shopping list (a *Rupture!*), so you have to improvise, which is not how you normally pick up groceries (*Newness*).

All this falls into the bucket of "little CHURN." It's unsettling, but the effects aren't permanent.

Figure 3: Defining CHURN

	Definition
CHANGE	A shift from one state to another
HICCUPS	Small delays and obstacles
UNCERTAINTY	Limited foresight into the future
RUPTURE	A sudden, surprising occurrence
NEWNESS	An unfamiliar experience

Figure 3. CHURN is an acronym for the varied events that test our AQ. Anything that disrupts the status quo is CHURN. Sometimes it is mildly frustrating; other times it is debilitating.

Then there's "big CHURN," which, unlike the minor, temporary nature of little CHURN, alters life in a meaningful way. In his book *Life Is in the Transitions,* Bruce Feiler calls these experiences "disruptors." Disruptors, Feiler says, run the gamut from seemingly positive moments, like getting married and graduating, to ones we'd rather avoid, like breakups, illnesses, or the death of a loved one.* He posits that, on average, we experience one new disruptor every twelve to eighteen

---

* You can find the full list of Feiler's disruptors at https://brucefeiler
.substack.com/p/the-deck-of-disruptors-21-08-11.

months. I resonate with Feiler's description of disruptors but wonder if they're now happening to us more often than he suggests. I've had a handful of my own this past year alone, and I'd be willing to bet it's the same for you. In today's increasingly unpredictable world, big CHURN has moved from the exception to the rule.

Figure 4: Little CHURN vs. Big CHURN

	Little CHURN	**Big CHURN**
Work/school	A canceled meeting New tools/software to learn Changes to a project Getting feedback	Graduating Starting/leaving a job Change in management Change in responsibilities
Relationships	Miscommunications Meeting new people Small arguments New shared experiences	Starting/ending a relationship Getting engaged/married Major conflict A new family member
Home	Weather events Minor repairs/broken appliances Uncomfortable living situations Personal travel	Moving Home renovations Major issues like pests and mold A new city/neighborhood
Well-being	Disturbances like a bad night's sleep New routines/habits Financial surprises Short-term illness	Major change in health Surgery or medical care Huge shifts in finances Changes in mindset or spirituality

Figure 4. CHURN is one of life's only constants. It is always happening to us whether we realize it or not. We experience little CHURN on a daily basis, and big CHURN, the events that permanently alter our lives, occur with surprising regularity, too.

Let's see how these concepts apply to your personal experience. What is an instance of little CHURN that you experienced today? Perhaps a meeting was canceled at the last minute, a project shifted scope, or it rained unexpectedly on your way home. What about big CHURN? What are the events that left an indelible mark on you this year?

Writing CHURN

One of my most memorable experiences of CHURN is when I spent several months writing my first book, *The Karma of Success*. On the surface, it seemed like I was excelling at the task. I strictly time-blocked my schedule and set up my days for optimal efficiency so I could continue to coach full-time. I put on identical clothes every day and ate from one pot of soup for breakfast, lunch, and dinner. I said no to every social invitation and set weekly word-count goals. (Remember, my Archetype is the Novelist, so I love making proactive plans.) At six weeks out from my deadline, I was exactly on track with 80 percent of the book written.

To celebrate nearing the finish line, I flew to my friend's house on the West Coast for a final writing sprint as she worked on her own book. Although all looked well on the surface, underneath was a different story. My book had no through line, lacked insight, and wasn't compelling. Somewhere, deep down, I knew my writing was subpar, but with a looming due date, I pushed this thought away because starting over seemed impossible. So, I continued to plow forward on the same dead-end road.

Shunryu Suzuki is right. *Everything changes,* and despite my best efforts, the plan I'd created for my book hadn't worked. We've all experienced some version of this. Perhaps you realize that a work project isn't feasible when you're already four months in. Or a long-term goal, like getting married or having children, has eluded you. When we face this unwanted and unplanned CHURN, we have three choices for how we can react, and each one correlates to a Stage of AQ. Here are the options for how we can respond:

Everything changes, and I resist it—This is the **Avoidant Stage** and the lowest form of agility.

Everything changes, and I deal with it—This is the **Fighting Stage**, a battle against CHURN.

Everything changes, and I embrace it—This is the **Full AQ Stage**, the highest form of agility.

In the first months of writing my book, I was stuck in the Avoidant Stage, resisting what was so obvious. The signs were there, bright and flashing, telling me to stop and try a new tack. But I didn't. In fact, I kept my self-delusion up for many months until I couldn't deny the truth any longer. To explore how and why this resistance happens to us, let's look at the Stages of AQ in detail.

Before we begin, I'd like to note that we humans are organic beings, inconsistent by nature, so it's normal to vacillate between the Stages in the same week, the same situation, or even the same minute. As you learn about the Stages, don't berate yourself if you've been stuck in the Avoidant Stage or the Fighting Stage for a long time. That's okay. The goal of AQ isn't perfection but improvement. Mastery is a product of continually noticing and adjusting your agility. This commitment to improvement is the embodiment of high AQ.

The Avoidant Stage

Most of us spend a large chunk of our lives in the Avoidant Stage, firmly in the grip of the status quo bias. In this state, we are determined to keep things as they are. Even when CHURN actively hammers us, we ignore the pain and pretend that everything is okay. For example, imagine that your workplace is evolving, with your co-workers pushing for a new company culture. In the Avoidant Stage, you chalk it up to a temporary fad and wait for things to go back as they were. You'll notice that *the Avoidant Stage is rigid.* It grips tightly to the status quo.

Next, consider a situation in which your partner has a fifty-fifty chance of getting laid off at the end of the quarter. In the Avoidant Stage, you don't face the issue head-on; instead, you distract yourself by watching extra TV and refilling your wineglass more than usual. You ignore the issue and deny that there is a problem. *The Avoidant Stage is withdrawn.* It turns a blind eye to what's obvious.

The Avoidant Stage doesn't just flare up in distinct situations like the ones above. It can also become your default way of approaching life. Perhaps it's been years since you changed your morning routine, hairstyle, or eating habits. Or you can't remember the last time you made new friends or work contacts. In the Avoidant Stage, the years pass, but the shape of your life remains unchanged. *The Avoidant Stage is stuck.*

We get trapped at the Avoidant Stage when we lack

confidence. We see the CHURN, but it's intimidating, and we don't believe we can handle it. We may see others around us changing, adapting, and stretching for what they want, but we think of ourselves as less than them, incapable of activating the same agility. Freeing yourself from the Avoidant Stage begins with building confidence in yourself and your ability to handle CHURN. You can start by returning to the practices in chapter 1. Explore your Archetype, take note of your strengths, and consider how you can apply them to become more confident. Let's see how this might work with one of the Archetypes.

More than any of their peers, Neurosurgeons are the most likely to get stuck in the Avoidant Stage. Remember, their strength is determination, but when it's applied in the wrong situations, this staying power turns into a weakness and keeps them stuck in old patterns. If you're a Neurosurgeon who is trapped in the Avoidant Stage, you can harness your strengths of discipline and diligence to craft a detailed plan that pushes you toward the future.

For example, if you're looking to switch industries, don't just set one big goal, like getting a new job in six months. Instead, create a regular, recurring target that makes agility a habit. Perhaps you commit to five new job applications a week or strive for monthly networking events. This will increase your comfort, and thus confidence, when it comes to making change. As you go about your plan, challenge yourself to feel at least 50 percent uncomfortable at all times. That discomfort will signal that you're on the right path and expanding your comfort zone.

Here's some direct advice for Neurosurgeons in the Avoidant Stage—loosen up your perfectionism, embrace trial and error, and realize that most decisions are less important than you imagine. Know that no matter how hard you try, you will inevitably stumble, but it will all be worth it because you're growing your AQ. You and your circumstances will change, whether you like it or not, so make a plan, do your best, and accept that life won't unfold perfectly, and that's okay.

No matter your Archetype, if you want to grow your AQ, you've got to get good at spotting when you're in the Avoidant Stage. To start, be on the lookout for moments when you've checked out of life. This includes escapism through substances like alcohol or distractions like working late or playing video games. Avoidance might look like isolating yourself from your friends and family or blaming others for your situation. The Avoidant Stage could also take the form of *displacement*, which means focusing on trivial matters instead of addressing the scary, important ones. That's what I do when I'm stuck in the Avoidant Stage. I've been known to fixate on my to-do list and push myself toward productivity, all the while ignoring the true challenges.

Once you notice what's going on, ask yourself one simple question: *What's the big, scary issue here?* And then you own up to what's happening, no matter how much you want to avoid it. Next, you fill your mind with a confident, high-AQ inner monologue that focuses on your strengths and assets. Soon enough, you will believe in yourself and your abilities, and you can move on to the next Stage of AQ.

The Fighting Stage

After spending most of my writing year in the Avoidant Stage, ignoring the call to change my book, I finally faced my big, scary issue on that trip to my friend's home. One late night, I admitted to her that I was disappointed by what I'd written. I told her about my desire to begin again, but of course, I said, that was a wild, impractical fantasy. As I relayed my many challenges, my friend listened quietly, and when I finished, she surprised me by telling me what to do. *Start over,* she said, and the look in her eyes held nothing but confidence in me. Her belief was the fuel I needed to start with a blank page, and it propelled me from the Avoidant Stage to the Fighting one.

This leap between Stages is meaningful, and it only happens once you've accumulated the confidence to go after what you want. It's a significant change because it moves you from inaction to action. You start pursuing what you want, and it's strenuous work. You are pulling, tugging, and using brute force to deal with CHURN. **Going from the Avoidant Stage to the Fighting Stage means that your AQ is growing, but so, too, is your discomfort.** You are evolving, which is a net positive, but it's an unpleasant experience. It certainly was tough for me.

I had a month and a half to write a brand-new book, and I had to do it amid a home renovation where construction was in full swing. There were no quiet spaces for me to work, very few walls, and even less internet because the previous owners never upgraded from a dial-up modem, and this made writing research impossible. To solve this problem, my husband bought a canvas camping tent, pitched it near the road (the only spot on the property with Wi-Fi access), and christened it my new office.

I was miserable in that tent. It was July, and the heat of the sun turned my "office" into a sauna where I sweat through my shirts. When thunderstorms hit, I clutched my computer and fled through the rain, terrified that the tent's metal pole in the flat field would be struck by lightning. Even in fine weather, there were hordes of daddy longlegs invading my space. I wondered why the world was conspiring against me, and why every day felt like a pummeling. I was taking action. I was changing the book, but every minute of it was pure torture. This was me, firmly ensconced in the Fighting Stage. In this Stage of AQ, we steel ourselves for battle, thinking "This is tough, but I am tougher," and we build our agility through hardship and toil. We finally accept CHURN after avoiding it for too long, but we certainly aren't having fun in the process.

Picture yourself in the Fighting Stage when it starts to rain on an idyllic hike through the woods. You rush back home, but you're drenched and annoyed, and you spend the afternoon in a bad mood. **When you're in the Fighting Stage, your thoughts are usually negative.** Here's another scenario: You miss out on the job you want, so you blame the company's interview process and get mad at yourself. **The Fighting Stage is critical (of yourself and others).** Imagine being in the Fighting Stage on your birthday, when you wake up with the flu. You've already planned your party, so you chug vitamins and try to sweat it out with a long walk. You tire yourself out by running around and become even sicker than before. **The Fighting Stage wastes energy.**

Of all the Archetypes, Firefighters are most prone to being in the Fighting Stage. After all, the word *fight* appears right in their name. As you'll recall, this Archetype is bold and resourceful. They're unintimidated by pressure and thrive even in pure chaos. They fight as a default and are better at it than anyone else. A Firefighter in the Fighting Stage is like a fish in the water. They excel at it, they're appreciated for it, and it's when they feel most useful.

But of course, there can always be too much of a good thing.

Nonstop fighting makes it hard to focus on other essential forms of agility work, like dreaming, planning, and resting. Firefighters are known to be behind on their accounting, late to appointments, and negligent about their long-term planning. Plus, somatically, the Fighting Stage takes a toll. It sends the nervous system into "fight or flight," leaving any person, no matter how skilled, feeling burnt-out and depleted.

Novelists, too, can fall easily into the Fighting Stage, but for different reasons than their Firefighter counterparts. For the Firefighter, the Fighting Stage is natural and instinctual. It's how they've been trained to deal with CHURN, and they happily step into this pugnacious way of being. Novelists, however, tumble unwillingly into the trap. Out of all the Archetypes, they are the planners, and they want it their way or the highway. Any detours send them into a spiral of negativity. CHURN makes them upset and pessimistic as they lament their fate. They keep moving, but they're unhappy, and that is the essence of the Fighting Stage.

To get out of the Fighting Stage, you might take a cue from Shunryu Suzuki, who said "Everything changes" without a hint of stress or anxiety. You can grow to accept unpleasant CHURN, like bad weather or traffic jams, as natural occurrences that eventually go away, and over time, by mastering AQ, you can even come to enjoy them. In order to move to the Full AQ Stage and reach the highest form of agility, you must adopt a brand-new mindset that sheds negativity and embraces optimism instead.

The Full AQ Stage

One day, after a particularly frustrating morning in my oven of an office-tent, I decided to drive to the small co-working space in town, where I could hopefully snag a private room and write without interruption. When I arrived, the only free desk was in the middle of the common area. I would be the first face anyone saw when they walked in.

My house is in a town of mostly retired residents who all know one another, so just as soon as I'd get into the writing flow, some well-meaning citizen would walk through the door with a friendly hello and jolt me from my focus. Around the tenth instance, I snapped and stormed out of the co-working space ready to cry but instead burst out laughing. I finally accepted that the writing process of my first book, which I had dreamed about for so long, was not going to look the way I had imagined it.

After lunch, I returned to my tent, which now seemed like an oasis after my day in town. I smiled at the daddy longlegs, grateful for how silent they were, and I decided to embrace them, giving the three nearest to me their own names—Derek, Deidre, and Dale. I looked at the sun shining through the canvas and the grass at my feet. It was different from what I'd planned, but I could recognize that it wasn't so bad. I was alive. I was writing for a living. I had a house and grass and daddy longlegs roommates. That day, I produced my best and favorite chapter of the book, and it only happened because I'd reached the Full AQ Stage. I was no longer fighting CHURN; instead, I was embracing it. I kept up this mindset, accepting whatever obstacles came my way, and finished in record time. I wrote an entire book in six weeks, and not only was I proud of what I'd written, but my editor was equally thrilled. The final product was a pleasant surprise to everyone, especially me.

When you inhabit the Full AQ Stage, you don't *resist change* as you do in the Avoidant Stage, or *deal with it* as you do in the Fighting Stage. Instead, you decide to find the good in whatever is happening and **embrace it**. The Full AQ Stage means that you stop asking "Why is this happening *to* me?" when things go wrong, and instead you consider "How might this be happening *for* me?" You become an expert at finding silver linings, no matter how unpleasant the CHURN. On the outside, how you behave in the Full AQ Stage may appear similar to what you do in the Fighting Stage. For instance, I worked hard on my writing in both Stages, but the difference was my mindset, which shifted from overwhelmed and beleaguered to positive and empowered. At the Full AQ Stage, there is lightness. Unlike being in the Fighting Stage, being in Full AQ feels good.

This shift to Full AQ is difficult to master because it requires intense mental gymnastics. Becoming the kind of person who can somersault over any hurdle with a big smile on their face is the opposite of what we've been taught. We want it easy. We want it sweet. We want smooth sailing and walks in the park. Reaching the Full AQ Stage requires flipping this preference on its head and instead realizing that easy isn't necessarily better, and not getting what you want might in fact be a win.

Let's revisit the scenarios we explored as we discussed the Fighting Stage, but now practice seeing them through the lens of Full AQ. When the rain starts pouring in the middle of your hike, soaking your clothes, you don't complain and push through. Instead, you focus on how important the rain is for the plants and flowers that you love so much, and how luscious they'll be tomorrow. **The Full AQ Stage is logical.**

When you miss out on the job you want, you don't blame the interviewers or yourself; instead, you parse through what you did well and what you could have improved. You take time to acknowledge the factors beyond your control. **The Full AQ Stage is unemotional.**

When you wake up feeling sick the morning of your birthday, you take this as a sign to rest. You feel lucky that you got sick on your birthday because now you have an open day to take it easy. **The Full AQ Stage is thankful.** Do you feel the difference between Full AQ, which is innately positive, and the Fighting Stage, which is negative?

Whenever I struggle to access the logical, unemotional, and thankful energy of the Full AQ Stage, it's helpful to reach out to my Astronaut friends. In fact, doing so made all the difference when I shared my oppressive writing fears with my friend in California. To find out if you know any Astronauts, share the Archetypes Quiz in chapter 1 with your closest companions and find out which of your friends might be floating around in space. If you still come up short, and there are no Astronauts at your disposal, turn to the people you know who easily can access the positive mindset of the Full AQ Stage, and specifically ask them to help you see your situation through an abundant lens. To be clear, this is not a promotion of toxic positivity, which goes beyond a positivity bias to encourage people to only acknowledge positive feelings at all times and to suppress negative ones. Of course, it is normal and necessary to express negative emotions about life's disappointments. In fact, it's the healthiest and most agile way to acknowledge and face these emotions. The Full AQ Stage does not deny these feelings. It simply confirms the importance of holding both the light and the dark at the same time. You can feel both sad *and* relieved. You can gripe *and* be grateful. Regret and pride can coexist in the same moment. No matter which Archetype you are, you're better when you learn to find the upsides amid CHURN.

Figure 5: The AQ Stages Summary

	"Everything Changes, and I . . ."	Qualities	The Antidote
Avoidant Stage	*Resist it*	Withdrawn, rigid, stuck	Build confidence.
Fighting Stage	*Deal with it*	Critical, negative, energy-wasting	Cultivate positivity bias.
Full AQ Stage	*Embrace it*	Logical, unemotional, thankful	

Figure 5. Every Stage of AQ is embodied by a specific mindset. In order to move up to the next Stage, you must first shift your mindset by leaning into the antidote, cultivating confidence and a positivity bias, until you arrive at the Full AQ Stage.

Now let's explore which of the Stages you've been spending the most time in. Think back to the most recent big CHURN you experienced. What Stage did you inhabit as you handled it? Did you ***resist*** it? Or did you ***deal with*** it? Perhaps you operated at Full AQ and ***embraced*** it. Maybe your response was a combination of all three. What is your default Stage, and how can you break free? Let's see how the Stages showed up in real life at Lex, a tech startup and social app for the LGBTQ+ community.

Lex Through the Stages

When Jennifer Lewis took over as the CEO of Lex, the company had already raised several million dollars in funding, despite showing little revenue. This wasn't unusual in 2023. In fact, many social apps that made zero money had even higher valuations. Lewis, who is structured and metrics-driven, created a plan to grow users and revenue in preparation for the company's Series A fundraise, their first major round of external investment.

Unfortunately, the tech investing market had its own plan, and just as Lewis kicked off her fundraising efforts the bar for Series A changed dramatically. Venture capital firms, which had become increasingly conservative over the previous year, were suddenly telling social apps that they needed at least $1 million in revenue to be considered for investment. Even though Lex had grown tremendously under Lewis's leadership, the company wasn't anywhere near that benchmark. Lewis had three options to choose from. Everything had changed, and she could either **resist it** (the Avoidant Stage), **deal with it** (the Fighting Stage), or **embrace it** (the Full AQ Stage). Initially, Lewis decided to ignore the market changes, because many of her advisors told her to stay strong. She brushed aside the chatter she'd heard around new expectations and pushed forward with her original goal. (This was the Avoidant Stage.)

It almost worked. Her dream investor was interested. He told her how much he believed in her and commended her for her leadership. Then, after several meetings, he passed. "Not enough revenue," he said. Shortly after, Lewis had yet another near win with an excited potential investor who also passed at the last minute. She was 0 for 2 and realized that resisting the market changes would not work. Lewis decided it was time for a new strategy, and she shifted to the Fighting Stage: Deal with it.

And deal with it, she did. Lewis launched new products to monetize the app, pushed her team to improve their metrics, and aggressively chased sponsorship opportunities. Then Lewis drew up an entirely new list of possible investors who might write smaller checks. She sent cold emails. She got warm intros. She took nonstop meetings, even working immediately before and after her grandmother's funeral. Lewis felt a tremendous responsibility to the Lex community and the employees who kept it going. She believed it would be her fault if the company failed, so even though she was exhausted from working eighty-hour weeks, she would not let herself rest. As we saw in figure 5, the Fighting Stage is *critical, negative, and energy-wasting*.

Anyone who knows Jennifer Lewis knows that she is ambitious, competitive, and relentlessly persistent. It's conceivable that she might have kept plowing down the path of the Fighting Stage, unwilling to change course until Lex was out of cash, she was fully burnt-out, and the app and community were shuttered. Instead, Lewis became open to a new strategy, and with the logical, unemotional, and thankful mindset of the Full AQ Stage, she decided to sell the company. Perhaps her inability to fundraise wasn't a failure, she realized, but an opportunity, and she took this positive outlook into her meetings with acquirers.

There are, of course, more twists and turns to this story, but in short, the acquisition was successful and Lewis sold Lex to a larger, well-funded creator of social apps whose founders and team she respects. Now she has the resources and ability to create products that Lex users care about, and the community so dear to her gets to live on. Over that year of tremendous CHURN, Lewis made her way up and down the Stages of AQ and back again. When she finally arrived at the highest setting, the Full AQ Stage, the sky burst open.

As you can see from Lewis's story, embracing Full AQ is a radical act. It requires you to stop fighting CHURN and to instead welcome it and trust it as it carries you into situations you never asked for. Of course, this new way of being takes practice. Our status quo bias is deeply entrenched, so conquering it won't happen overnight. If Full AQ doesn't feel natural to you right now, that's okay. Trust that you'll arrive there by the end of this book.

Summary of Part 1:
AQ Everywhere

The four Archetypes walk into a crowded bar. After two rounds of happy hour drinks, they pay their tab and head out the door. "Hey! You forgot your change," the bartender yells, and the Archetypes turn to respond, each in their own way.

The Firefighter is the first to rush back in and collect the money. She takes action before anyone else can. The Neurosurgeon double-checks the bill, counts the change, and ensures that each person gets the proper amount due. The Novelist is in his own world, preferring to daydream about dinner than deal with the hubbub in front of him. And the Astronaut? She's already gone, rushing to a concert down the street, ready for something new.

This light little anecdote illustrates how you'll begin to notice the Archetypes in every dimension of your life. You'll wonder about your family and friends, observing them for clues.

You'll recognize the Neurosurgeon's attention to detail in your cousin's DIY home repairs, and you'll clock your co-worker's imaginative event planning as a trait of the Novelist. Perhaps you'll actively explore these concepts with the people in your life, sharing a meal and a discussion about which Archetypes you are.

Then you'll come home, turn on your TV, and see the Archetypes on your screen. If you've ever watched *Seinfeld*, you'll recognize Jerry as the Neurosurgeon, with an analytical nature and high standards, while George, endlessly scheming to improve his future, is the Novelist. Elaine, the most practical and productive of them all, is the Firefighter, and of course, Kramer, known for his eccentric nature, is the Astronaut.

You'll see the Archetypes in real life, in books, on film, and even in music. (I always think about the Neurosurgeon when I hear "Someone Like You" by Adele.) I recently spent the holidays in California visiting my family, and I challenged myself to shop for Christmas presents with the Archetypes in mind. I picked up an Oliver Sacks book for my brother, the Neurosurgeon, who is diligently studying to become a therapist. My Astronaut aunt, who dreams of building a farm in Vermont, received a compendium of beautiful homes in the woods, and for my Firefighter husband, I picked out a German steel axe for the cleanup work he does on our property in the wake of big storms. I'm not one for shopping, but framed through the lens of AQ, a boring task transformed into a stimulating education.

The Stages came in handy over that holiday season, too. At the end of every delightful yet taxing day, short on childcare and long on logistics, I sat down with a mug of tea to reflect on my day, asking myself what Stage of AQ I inhabited. The first few days in L.A., I behaved as I would pre-child, and I over-scheduled our appointments to my family's detriment. With an Avoidant Stage mindset, I hadn't acknowledged that our circumstances had changed. Then we took a train down to San Diego, scheduled to coincide with my daughter's nap time. When she refused to sleep, I worked overtime to keep her entertained and recognized the frustration of the Fighting Stage within myself. Then, when my brother locked his keys inside the house and derailed our family trip to the zoo, I embraced the CHURN with the positive attitude of Full AQ. With the Stages always on my mind, I had a clear yardstick by which to measure my own agility.

Now your goal is to bring the Archetypes and Stages into your own life, too, especially in the most ordinary moments. Even with just one day of practice, you'll see that your world gains richness and depth, and this, in turn, makes you deeper. You'll have more empathy and patience for the people around you, and you'll be able to see yourself—strengths, challenges, and all—with high fidelity.

As an executive coach, I'm a stickler for ideas that you'll return to again and again, so if you take anything from part 1 of this book, let it be this:

Agility Belief #1: Everything changes, and I embrace it.

Agility Belief #2: I love change, and change loves me.

These two short sentences are a simple way to enshrine everything we've just learned. Use these beliefs as a filter for your thoughts, sifting out the detritus of the Avoidant and the Fighting Stages to reveal the logical and thankful mindset of Full AQ.

Now that we've explored your personality through the Archetypes and the Stages, we enter part 2 of the book, "What You Think," where we'll venture into the terrain of *mindset* with the ABC's, four tools that equip you to see the world through agile eyes.

PART 2

What You Think

All that we are is the result of
what we have thought.

—The Buddha

Keiko's ABC's

Just as a human child must learn the rules of their world, orcas, those sleek black-and-white members of the dolphin family, learn from their elders, too. Like us, they have names. They have language. They form yearslong friendships outside of their family, and they use these connections to survive and thrive. If you want to be an orca, you must grow up with other orcas.

What if you never had that opportunity? What if you, like an orca named Keiko, who is better known as the star of the 1993 film *Free Willy*, were kidnapped from your family as a baby and shuttled for almost two decades from amusement park to amusement park and then to a movie set? What if you were isolated, forced to exist only for the entertainment of another species? Could you, as a young adult, return to human society and function successfully?

These are questions that researchers who study captive cetaceans (whales, dolphins, and porpoises) have been pondering for years. Can these impressively intelligent animals be rewilded?

How much can they learn and change? What are the limits of their agility, and how much guidance, direction, and support should humans give them to transition back to their native but forgotten environment?

There is so much we can learn from animals while we try to increase our own agility. After all, most our own experiences of CHURN pale against the concerns of animals like Keiko. "Rehabilitating a formerly captive whale is nothing like the triumphant leap to freedom in 'Free Willy,'" journalist Ferris Jabr writes. "It's more like helping a severely traumatized victim of abduction reintegrate with society." If we study how our mammalian relatives can accomplish feats of AQ far more intense than what we'll ever face, perhaps we can learn critical and effective lessons for the more manageable CHURN we humans encounter.

You might be wondering about what happened to Keiko. Did he ever make it back to the wild sea like his onscreen counterpart? Life is always more complex than fiction, and Keiko was not prepared to go back to sea. Because Keiko was raised by people, he was more like a human toddler than a wild animal. He played with toys. He watched cartoons on TV. He preferred eating frozen fish over fresh, and he was afraid of other orcas. Keiko was not a strong swimmer because he looped around in small aquarium circles, and unlike most sea creatures, he couldn't hold his breath for very long. What was the plan to get him from mild to wild? How would his trainers and caretakers pull off this incredible feat of agility?

In the previous section of this book, "Who You Are," we explored your *personality*—the Archetype that defines you, and the strengths and weaknesses that impact your agility. Now we'll explore the terrain of *mindset*, with the ABC's of Agility, which are the primary tools for increasing your AQ. When you learn these tools, you change the way you perceive and respond to CHURN, raising your agility in the process. Before we go deeper in the next chapters, I'll give you a quick overview of the ABC's now, using Keiko's experience.

A Is for *Anchors*

The first tool is called *anchors,* so let's consider what an anchor is. For a boat, it's a point of stability in unsteady seas, and the same holds true for our own lives. Anchors are what steady us in the turbulence of CHURN. Like those iron weights that tether ships to the sea floor, our own anchors are the **people, places, and routines that ground our lives.** Comforting and familiar, they help us stay calm in the roughest of seas.

During Keiko's rehabilitation, he lived for four years in a sea pen on Heimaey, an island in Iceland. It was 250 feet long, far larger than the tanks he'd lived in, and surrounded by grass that grew above the volcanic rock, where the local sheep would graze. These were years of great CHURN for Keiko, as his trainers pushed him hard to learn orca life, and even more so when the money for his rehabilitation dwindled. Still, no matter how arduous the day, Keiko could always return to the comfort of his pen. It was his anchor. The more change, uncertainty, and unknown we face in our lives, the more anchors we need to steady ourselves.

B Is for *Bets*

The next letter is *B,* which stands for *bets.* Like a spin of the roulette wheel in the hope of winning money, **a bet means taking action,**

despite not knowing the outcome. It's a wish, a risk. It's a chance we take on ourselves. Keiko's ocean walks were his bets. On these sojourns, he'd follow his trainer's boat as he explored the open sea for the first time as an adult. Every walk held surprises, including birds that scared him and wild orcas that rejected him. However unknown and uncertain these bets were, they allowed Keiko to stretch his agility and expand the aperture of his universe.

C Is for *Classroom*

This next tool is called *classroom*, and as you can probably infer, it's about learning. This type of learning goes deeper than reading a book, listening to a podcast, or even going back to school. It's all-encompassing. To master this tool, **you turn your whole world into a classroom, where anything that transpires is a teachable moment.**

There was so much for Keiko to learn. He'd never hunted before, never fed himself. He didn't even know how to pec slap, which is basic orca communication. Keiko's trainers worked through a daunting list of skills to acquire, like diving, blowing bubbles, and retrieving objects from deep in the ocean. His trainers were learning, too. No one had ever tried to rehabilitate and release a captive cetacean before. The entire experiment, for everyone involved, was one giant classroom in the ocean off Iceland.

D Is for *Discomfort*

This final tool is the hardest for many people. After all, it's about learning to do the opposite of our instincts and seek out *discomfort,* which we define as **any challenging and uncomfortable feelings or sensations.** When we truly live this tool, we evolve our relationship with discomfort until our initial instincts are flipped on their head. Instead of avoiding it, we accept it, knowing that it is the clearest sign that we are becoming more agile.

Keiko's entire rehabilitation experience was an exercise in discomfort. His new home was colder, windier, and rougher than the enclosed spaces he knew. He missed people. Gone were the adoring visitors and the kids to whom he'd given rides on his back. Over time, Keiko's trainers stopped talking to him, thinking this would foster independence, and at points they avoided eye contact. This was painful for an orca who was raised as a human. This tool addresses a fundamental truth—progress is hard. There is no change, no newness, no unknown that is not also accompanied by strain, but in mastering it, we accept it and recognize discomfort as a harbinger of good things to come.

CHAPTER 3

Anchors Aweigh

Be like the rocky headland
on which the waves constantly break.
It stands firm, and round it the
seething waters are laid to rest.

—Marcus Aurelius

After Carla Fernandez's father passed away when she was twenty-one, a single source of steadiness grounded her more than any other. Was it the grief counselor at the hospital, offering brochures of guidance for the bereaved? Was it the brain cancer support group that gathered beneath fluorescent lights in the hospital basement? Or was it the vibrant memorial for her father, as spirited and full of life as he had been? Carla's crucial anchor was none of these. It was far more unassuming. Her anchor was her family recipe for arroz con pollo, which she cooked up in a big batch and served to a small circle of friends who, like her, had known loss at a young age.

That's the quiet power of anchors: They are as simple as they are profound. They form the backbone of our lives, so consistent and present that we often take them for granted. **Anchors are the people, places, and routines that offer the stability we need to be agile.** Picture a tree, its branches thrashing in the wind. It can withstand the turbulence only because of its deep, resilient roots. We are no different: The greatest agility is made possible by the strongest foundations. In fact, the more CHURN we face, the more essential our anchors become. When we nurture them, as Carla did, they become powerful, life-shaping forces.

Figure 6: Types of Anchors

People	Places	Routines
• Neighbors	• Nature and greenspaces	• Daily commute
• Communities	• Schools	• Cooking and meals
• Organizations	• Museums	• Sleep habits
• Colleagues	• Libraries	• Movement and exercise
• Friends	• Places of worship	• Leisure and fun
• Family members	• Workplaces	• Date nights
• Romantic partners	• Community centers	• Reading
• Business partners	• Sports centers	• Tending to home
• Mentors and mentees	• Current home	• Pets
• Therapists	• Childhood home	• Self-care
• Coaches	• Someone else's home	• Meditation and prayer

Figure 6. Anchors are the people, places, and routines that provide grounding to our lives in times of CHURN. Anchors are comforting, stabilizing, and nourishing.

People Anchors

We all instinctively understand the grounding power of human connection. A hug soothes, a conversation brings relief. When we are lost and overwhelmed, even the briefest moments of support can restore clarity. No matter how independent we may be, we all need others—especially during periods of intense CHURN, when we can't find stability on our own.

This grounding happens on a broader scale, too. Research on natural disasters shows that communities with stronger social ties are more agile and recover faster, with the members stepping up to serve as one another's anchors. When Hurricane Sandy struck New York in 2012 and left almost a million people without power for ten days, it was powerful to witness New Yorkers, known for their solitary brusqueness, unite in compassion in the wake of the storm.

Elizabeth Duffy from Queens recalls how strangers rallied around her community, arriving with food, tents, clothing, building supplies, and gift cards. "These people came to the yacht club and handed out these little wool gray scarfs," she said. "It was the warmest scarf I've ever had." A decade later, when Hurricane Ian ravaged the Florida coast, Elizabeth felt it was her turn to become an anchor for others. She organized donations from neighbors and collected $5,000 worth of gift cards. Then she and her sister drove eighteen hours to Florida to help another community rebuild their homes. Elizabeth hoped to pay forward the kindness, generosity, and anchoring that she had once received.

A few years ago, while struggling through IVF and fearing I might never become a parent, a near stranger reached out to me—she had walked a similar path and offered to talk. Over tea and breakfast, Piera shared her long journey to parenthood and listened deeply to my own unfinished story. By breakfast's end, something had shifted. I felt hope again. Piera was the anchor I needed to believe in possibility.

Over time, our relationship deepened, and she was the first friend I called when I found out I was pregnant. "I'm having a baby!" I shouted, and we jumped up and down in our respective apartments across the Williamsburg Bridge. "I want to read you something," Piera said, and she took out a book called *On the Day You Were Born.* Her mother had read it to her every year on her birthday, and she continued that tradition with her own daughter. That day, she read it for mine: just a poppy-seed-sized ball of cells, but finally, miraculously real. Piera's gentle voice narrated the pages, and we both cried while the stars, trees, and animals in the story rejoiced at the arrival of a long-awaited baby. Piera is my confidante, role model, and supporter. She is an anchor no matter how rough the seas.

In many ways, I see myself as an anchor for my clients, a constant and grounding presence, much like Piera is for me. I've worked with most of them for years, through setbacks, missteps, and crises of confidence. I've witnessed them falter and crash, question themselves and their decisions. And yet, because I am their anchor, my belief in them never wavers. I am always there, no matter the time of night or the day of the week. I hold a steady vision of who they are at their best and guide them back to it again and again.

Not long ago, I spoke to a startup founder who is building AI clones of executive coaches to help them scale the one-on-one nature of their businesses. At first, I was hesitant, even offended. How could an algorithm replicate the affinity and nuance of my coaching practice? How could a chatbot replace the genuine care

I express for my clients? But then I remembered the importance of cultivating AQ, and I decided to stay open to learning more.

"Imagine," he said, "in just four to six weeks, with just ten hours of your time, we can build an AI clone of you with your memory, your references, and your exact coaching methodology. It could run client sessions exactly as you do, and you could make money doing nothing." It was an interesting proposition. As a knowledge worker who bills by the hour, I found the idea of generating passive income at scale appealing. "We can even make your clone sound like you," he added, "unless you think that's creepy."

But I didn't think it was creepy. I'm a realist. I accept that I'm imperfect, far more imperfect than an AI model, and I know that the technology of the future is coming not just for my job but for all our jobs. Yet there was still something about the setup that didn't make sense, and when I dug in further, I understood that it's about *people anchors.* Yes, I believe that my AI clone could mirror the mechanics of what I do—posing thoughtful questions, sharing case studies, and synthesizing ideas. In fact, I'm excited to explore what AI can do for coaching. But it will never surpass the profound privilege of receiving unconditional care from a people anchor. That kind of grounding is transformative, and no algorithm can replace it.

The more we come to rely on technology for our daily tasks, responsibilities, and decision-making, the more we need to invest in our human-to-human interactions, those bonding ties that connect us to other people. We are at the precipice of a future where none of us will ever need to drive our own cars, write our own emails, or brush our own teeth because machines will do it for us, but what will never change is our need for one another. We humans, no matter how far removed we become from our origins, are tribal creatures, and we will always appreciate and yearn for those personal interactions that keep us tethered to solid ground.

Ironically, we especially neglect to reach out to our people anchors when we need them most. Either we feel too busy and overwhelmed to add another event to our calendar, or we think no one wants to hear from us when we're in a bad mood. Know this bias exists and push yourself. Hold yourself accountable to meeting with your mentor every quarter, whether you think you need to or not. When you want to wallow in sadness alone, ask a friend to go for a walk anyway. When you're sure your parent won't understand what you're going through, give it a shot and call them. My husband and I go to bed at different hours. I prefer to be in my pajamas by ten, and he stays awake as late as possible. When I'm in times of CHURN, I ask for a nighttime routine. We hang out and chat as we get ready for sleep together. Then we turn out the light, I close my eyes, and he slips out of bed to continue his night. It's my favorite part of the day. We only get the anchoring we need if we ask.

THE ARCHETYPES AS ANCHORS

The simplest way to become a steady anchor is to lean into your Archetype.

Take Piera, for instance, who anchored me through IVF. She is an **Astronaut,** and true to form, she instills *courage* in those around her. When you're feeling hopeless or lost, as I once did, there is no better support than the Astronaut. They don't just pull you out of the fog—they lift you into the stratosphere, where together you can float with lightness and perspective. If you're an

Astronaut who wants to anchor someone you love, let them draw strength from your confidence and sense of mission.

I, on the other hand, am a **Novelist,** and my Archetype serves as an anchor through *planning*. I read my friends' cover letters and résumés. I inquire about their five-year plans and their quarterly goals. Anytime I'm with loved ones, I instinctively take charge of the logistics—setting the schedule, tracking the time, and ensuring everyone's needs are considered. Novelists like me, who specialize in Proactive Change, express support through clarity and structure. If you're a Novelist, too, you become the best anchor you can be by helping your loved ones get organized.

Firefighters, by contrast, anchor through *problem-solving*. Experts in Reactive Change, they show up for others by reacting swiftly and decisively when things go wrong. I watch my husband embody this daily. From morning to night, he fields calls from employees with issues, which he calmly resolves, and he is the go-to person for friends in the midst of emergencies or career crises. If you're a Firefighter like him, your greatest impact as an anchor comes when you step unflinchingly into moments of challenge.

Then there are the **Neurosurgeons,** arguably the most grounding of all the Archetypes, with their superpower of unwavering *loyalty*. Neurosurgeons show up with effort and consideration. They'll cook your favorite meal, leave handwritten notes of encouragement, and never forget your birthday, no matter where in the world they are. In short, Neurosurgeons *care*. If you're a Neurosurgeon and you want to be your best anchor, simply be who you are. Your mere presence is stabilizing to everyone around you.

Whatever your Archetype, I encourage you to deepen your

role of anchor this week by meeting a friend or family member on their own terms. Choose a hobby or an activity that they hold dear and join them in it. Make it your mission to be even more engaged and curious than they are in the moment. This small effort to walk in your loved one's shoes will feel profoundly grounding—for them and likely for you, too.

Place Anchors

One place you can reliably find me is on my couch, marathoning episodes of my guilty pleasure, a show called *Alone*, in which homesteaders and survivalists battle it out with the remote Canadian wilderness, hunting, foraging, and fishing with no more than ten items in their packs. They boil reindeer moss to stave off hunger pangs. They ice-fish, soft bellies pressed against the frozen lake, and skin squirrels for scant bites of meat clinging to translucent bones. The strategy is clear: Secure the most food while expending the fewest calories. These men and women are savvy and experienced in living off the land. They know better than to waste their precious time and energy on building elaborate shelters, but they just can't help themselves.

They haul felled tree trunks with their bare hands and then carve them notch by notch until they become cabins. They design welcome signs and build chessboards and construct easy chairs from sticks. They put so much heart into crafting not just a shelter but a real home. "Save your strength!" I scream at the TV, knowing that winter is approaching, and it would be more prudent to take down a moose instead of nesting. But, as the show's name implies, each contestant goes at it by themselves, *alone*, without any companions to support them, so bereft of their peo-

ple anchors that they seek solace in another source of security—
a *place anchor.*

Psychologically, this makes perfect sense. According to
Maslow's hierarchy of needs—a foundational model of human
motivation—we must satisfy our most basic necessities before we
can realize more advanced desires. At the very base of the pyra-
mid are essentials including air, water, food, and of course shelter. Every person, *Alone* contestants included, needs a place that is
safe, secure, and stable. We know that there is an intrinsic connection between shelter and spirit. It's the relief of coming home,
and the anxiety of being untethered. Countless studies confirm
the connection between unstable housing and cognitive overload.
When we are worried about where we are, we cannot focus on
where we are going.

During my IVF journey, I felt this need for spatial grounding
acutely. A few years earlier I had moved into a sun-drenched,
floor-through apartment impeccably renovated by its artist owners. Though it sat atop seventy-two stairs and was in a less-than-
desirable neighborhood, the below-market price made it seem
like a Manhattan miracle—and for a time, it was. I hosted friends,
threw dinner parties, and turned the spacious third bedroom into
my office. It was a happy time.

Then almost overnight, the neighborhood changed. My
block became a hub for drug activity, and the sense of home I'd
built there vanished. One day, I saw a news alert: A neighbor, an
Asian American woman in her thirties, like me, had been mur-
dered just three blocks away. Not long after, I was punched in the
ear one Sunday morning while walking my dog, and soon I was
accustomed to stepping over limp, unconscious bodies just to
leave my building. My home no longer felt like a refuge.

With my personal sanctuary gone, I began seeking stability

elsewhere, setting out on long walks to different New York City parks, letting the trees and open air soothe my frayed nervous system. Of course, a home can be an ultimate anchor, but when that's not possible, Full AQ asks us to adapt: to accept the reality and search for places where grounding is possible. It might be your workplace, a favorite coffee shop, a friend's backyard, or a quiet tree-lined block with a bench. I've found anchors in all those places. At the best place anchors, you see others drawn there, too, returning regularly to meet the same need for grounding. There are no fixed rules for what makes a place an anchor—it simply needs to feel safe and stable. That said, I've found the most enduring ones tend to be rich in love, history, earth, or spirit.

Jonathan Slon's apartment on the Upper West Side of Manhattan has all those qualities in spades. It is a rare gem—a rent-controlled apartment with no significant rate increase since 1938, when his grandparents moved in. Not only has this four-bedroom apartment housed five generations of his family, but it's also sheltered countless international students from countries like Japan, France, and Taiwan who found themselves far from the security of their home countries and surrounded by CHURN. Slon's family always let them stay there for free. One of these students, Adnan Brankovich, was a seventeen-year-old Bosnian war refugee when he moved in, and he stayed there with Slon and his wife, whom he calls his "American parents," for five years. The Slons don't hoard their anchor for themselves; instead, they share it widely and openly.

A special quality of anchors is that they multiply goodwill. Kindness and support are not only given but also paid forward magnanimously, over and over again. In New York City, there are only about 24,020 rent-controlled units out of almost 4 million apartments, making Jonathan Slon's situation a true blessing. He and the rest of his kin recognize the good luck they've had with their simple family mantra: "Make good use of the space." They've done so repeatedly by helping others to find their footing.

Carla Fernandez, who cooked arroz con pollo for her friends after her father died, eventually did the same with her anchor. After seeing how these meals did so much good for young grievers, she started a not-for-profit organization called The Dinner Party. Since 2014, it's connected more than sixteen thousand people across one hundred cities to process their grief over a shared meal. The lesson here is this: When you find your anchor, don't just hold on tight—invite others in, too, and the stability you feel will only multiply in the process.

Routine Anchors

During those difficult years of trying—and failing—to get pregnant, I leaned heavily on people and place anchors because both offered a sense of steadiness I could not find on my own. But what made the greatest difference were my *routine anchors*— the activities, habits, and rituals that brought structure and a sense of control to an unpredictable chapter of my life.

I had a notebook expressly for this purpose. Each month, I'd draw a simple grid, one small square for each day, and give myself a moment of satisfaction each night by checking the box if I'd upheld my four commitments: eat healthily, take vitamins, move my body, and go to bed on time. I wasn't sculpting bonsai or training for an Ironman. These weren't grand undertakings, but they brought much-needed order to a life that felt otherwise chaotic.

I had other routine anchors, too. An afternoon cup of tea. A stick of incense before doctor's appointments. At night, a short visualization: me walking barefoot through thick, dewy grass and looking down at a beach-ball belly. Each of these took less than a minute, but they mattered. Now think about your own life. Chances are, you already have a few routine anchors. Perhaps in your commute, your snacks, or your rituals at the start and end of the day. Again, a routine anchor doesn't need to be profound or ambitious. It just needs to be regular, because in its predictability, we find peace.

Remember Jennifer Lewis from chapter 2, who found herself scaling up the Stages of AQ as she tried to save her company, Lex? She held to her routine anchors during this time. In the rare minutes between meetings and emails, Jennifer organized her home, which was itself a place anchor for her. After fourteen-hour workdays, she forced herself to decompress at yoga class. When Jennifer's team was let go, leaving her solely responsible for their email inboxes, she tackled the flood of messages with daily focus. Her routine anchors became something dependable when the future seemed so unclear.

In fact, all my clients, in one way or another, rely on routine anchors. One turns to long bike rides; the more stressful work becomes, the more distance he covers. During the hardest moments of building his company, he also taught himself to play the piano. At first glance, it may seem counterintuitive to enjoy leisure time when work is all-consuming, but these anchors didn't drain his time or attention—they sharpened it. They grounded him, restored his energy, and made him a better CEO. Symbolically, the piano offers something rare: proof that effort leads to progress. Dedicate a few minutes each day to learning a piece, and inevitably you will perfect it. There's not much else in life we can rely on for that sort of fated success. In a world where outcomes are rarely guaranteed, a steady, reliable return is precious, and our routine anchors give us that gift.

While I struggled with IVF, I leaned most on routine anchors, but that won't hold true for everyone. Some of us favor people anchors, while others prefer to be grounded by places. There is no right formula. What matters is that you find the precise combination of anchors that works for you.

The good news is that most of us already have anchors—we just haven't named them. Let's try it together now. Take a moment to scan your life. Who or what grounds you, even in the smallest way? A person. A place. A practice. Perhaps it's a cup of coffee at the same time each morning or a conversation that brings you back to yourself. Now pause and truly see these people, places, and things for what they are: anchors. When we recognize and appreciate them, we strengthen their effect.

Anchors are the most intuitive of all the agility ABC's, yet ironically we forget to reach for them just when we need them most. We're too stressed to call a loved one, too busy to tidy up, and too overwhelmed to follow our routine. Fortunately, this pattern can be easily broken with simple self-awareness. Now that you know about anchors, you can commit to them in any moment of CHURN. The best part? The most powerful anchors are the ones already in place. You've built them. You know them. All that's left is to see them, name them, and relish in their security.

ANCHORS EXERCISE

What grounds you when you're lost at sea?

- Write down one **person** who is an anchor in your life. Connect with them in some way.

- Write down one **place** where you feel safe, secure, and stable. How can you spend more time there?

- Write down some **routines** you already engage in that could be anchors if you named and empowered them. How can you commit to a daily practice?

- What is one anchor that you can share with others?

CHAPTER 4

Wanna Bet?

Sometimes your only available
transportation is a leap of faith.

—Margaret Shepard

Let's begin this chapter with a version of the classic icebreaker game Would You Rather.

Imagine you get a job offer, and you have two choices for your compensation. Would you pick:

A. A fixed annual salary of $50,000

B. A base salary of $40,000 and a bonus that ranges from nothing to $30,000 based on both your performance and the company's performance

You're swiping on a dating app looking for a serious relationship. Would you rather go on a date with:

A. Someone with detailed information and clear photos

B. Someone you're curious about but there's not much information

You fall in love and want to celebrate your anniversary with a long weekend trip. Do you prefer:

A. To go somewhere that was highly recommended by a friend

B. To go somewhere you don't know anything about

Ten years from now, you find out that you have a rare medical condition. Luckily, it can be treated. Do you prefer:

A. The traditional treatment with a 50 percent chance of success and known side effects

B. A newer, experimental treatment with a 30–80 percent chance of success and unknown side effects

If you answered *A* most often, then you're not alone. That's your innate **Ambiguity Aversion** at play. Ambiguity Aversion is a psychological bias that favors *known* risk over *unknown* risk, even if the unknown might be the superior choice. Ambiguity Aversion explains the old saying "Better the devil you know than the devil you don't." We're drawn to what's familiar, even at our own expense. Ambiguity Aversion keeps us clinging to the known and hinders our AQ.

Ambiguity Aversion has deep evolutionary roots, dating back to our hunter-gatherer ancestors who spent their days foraging for food. The ones with *low* Ambiguity Aversion would take risks on mysterious berries and mushrooms, only to discover their poisonous nature too late. End scene for our risk-taking forefathers. The hunter-gatherers who were more cautious, sticking to the flora they knew, were the ones with *high* Ambiguity Aversion. They survived long enough to pass on their genes, which eventually landed with us.

Today, we don't face the same dangers. Our food is processed and genetically modified, and if I snap a photo of berries or mushrooms, an app will tell me if they're poisonous. Our daily decisions don't carry the same life-or-death weight, but still, as we saw in the Would You Rather game, our intolerance for the unknown hasn't changed. We like what's familiar. We want guarantees. We keep our worlds small instead of venturing into the great unknown. If you want to expand your world and increase your AQ, this must change. You must become comfortable with ambiguity and learn to embrace the unfamiliar. You do this through the second mindset of the ABC's—by learning how to bet.

Bets Defined

A bet is an action you take without knowing the outcome. It's stepping into unfamiliar terrain. It's a dance with mystery. Put simply, it's trying something new. A bet means moving forward without certainty—whether you're changing your shirt or changing your city. Bets are any behaviors, no matter their scope, that feel different, uncertain, or unfamiliar. They are the antidote for Ambiguity Aversion. They disrupt entrenched habits and break open your world.

Betting is also one of the efficient ways to grow your AQ. As you know from chapter 2, when you're in the Avoidant Stage, you're resisting CHURN and denying reality. You're stuck in the same place you've always been. You convince yourself that there's no problem and therefore nothing you should do differently. But the moment you place a bet, you break free from that inertia. You're launched out of the stagnation of the Avoidant Stage into the forward momentum of the Fighting Stage. You shift from avoidant to engaged, immobile to in motion, and this is nothing short of transformative.

Bets need not be risky or terrifying. Of course, there are perilous ones like BASE jumping, high-risk day-trading, or gambling one's savings, but the bets that we should care about are the reasonable ones. They are low-stakes choices like saying hi to a stranger, taking up jogging, or raising your hand for more responsibility at work. These bets may be small, but their importance is huge because, when done with regularity, betting makes you comfortable with the unknown, erases your Ambiguity Aversion, and raises your AQ.

Figure 7: Types of Bets

Small Bets/Low Stakes	Big Bets/High Stakes
• Wearing something unexpected	• Getting married
• Trying out someone else's advice	• Having children
• Expressing your feelings	• Coming out
• Negotiating or asking for a discount	• Taking a career leap
• Stating your opinion when you're afraid to	• Starting a new business
• Proposing a change to an existing system	• Buying a home
• Disagreeing with someone you like	• Moving to a new area
• Sharing creative work	• Taking action against a powerful entity
• Doing the opposite of what you normally do	• Confronting an addiction
• Consuming something new, such as food, drink, entertainment, or books	• Going public with a vulnerability
	• Setting new boundaries in a dynamic

Figure 7. Bets are the actions we take without knowing the outcome. Because of our innate Ambiguity Aversion, making bets can feel nerve-racking, even when the stakes are objectively low.

Bet Hopefully

When we think about relationships, we can romanticize them as something fated and inevitable—meant to be, if you will. This was certainly *not* the case for my husband and me. In fact, nothing about our love story felt predestined. Had we both played it safe, I am convinced that we would not be married today. Thankfully, we took risks and bet on each other, even when it was uncomfortable, and those small leaps of faith got us here today.

One of our early bets came just a few weeks into dating: We

decided to cross the Atlantic Ocean together—on a cargo ship. The idea emerged after a few glasses of wine, and in the moment it seemed exhilarating and romantic. But by the next morning, reality had set in. The trip would require us to spend seven to ten days together (depending on the ocean current), with no cell service, no internet, and almost no other passengers.

Dev and I barely knew each other. We'd been on a handful of dates, mostly dinners, but I hadn't met his friends, peered into his pantry, or stayed over at his apartment. He liked his space, and I liked mine. The cargo ship would upend all that. We'd be confined to a small room with a desk and two single beds, with no one else to talk to and nothing to do for twenty-four hours a day. There were countless reasons not to go—and I came up with many. In fact, I nearly canceled the trip two days before sailing. I called a friend in a panic, flooded with what-ifs. *What if I discover I don't like him? What if he doesn't like me? What if we want to break up, but we're stuck in the middle of the ocean?* There were so many unknowns, and they sent my Ambiguity Aversion into overdrive.

It turns out the trip was even harder than I'd imagined. Our room smelled of sewage, I fell ill during the last half, and—since I was vegan at the time—there was very little for me to eat. Most challenging of all, Dev and I had different understandings of how we wanted to spend our time, and this led to our first real fight. Still, I am grateful that I didn't back out, because we fell in love on that cargo ship. The long, empty days gave us time to talk—really talk—and the bare-bones environment revealed that we could be happy anywhere, together. On that ship, we began to imagine our life as partners. That same year, Dev helped me switch careers and start my own business. Then, when that business shut down in the pandemic, he packed the boxes, dealt with the movers, and let me cry on the floor as I mourned the death of my dream. Today, he makes me laugh, he reads my drafts, and he spends every morning with our daughter so I can sleep in.

It pains me to remember that I almost backed out. I wanted to go. I was excited, but I was also afraid, stuck in a spiral of negative what-ifs. In that moment, I could choose either **hope** or **fear.** And that's the same choice all of us face, every time we bet. We call these two choices *hopeful bets* and *hedging bets.*

Hopeful bets are optimistic, expansive, and energizing. They focus on what could go *right.* Hedging bets are cautious, self-protective, and fear-based. They focus on what could go *wrong.* In finance, hedging is a common strategy for limiting risk. You don't fully invest in any area. Instead, you spread out your interests to protect against downside. Outside of investing, we humans hedge all the time. We hold ourselves back from hoping, from trying, from caring too much—thinking that if we don't get our hopes up, we won't be disappointed.

If I had canceled the cargo ship trip, it would have been a hedging bet—a way to protect myself from potential heartbreak. But I also would have missed the chance to fall in love. The lesson is this: ***Hedging bets might protect you, but they also keep you from what you truly want.***

To bet and to bet well, you must make hopeful bets. After all, the entire point of betting is to expand your world with newness and change. We only build AQ by betting on growth, not on safety. So, the next time you are at a crossroads, pause and ask yourself: ***What's the hopeful bet? What's the hedging bet?*** Then choose the former. Board your own version of the cargo ship, because it's the hopeful bets that stretch us, shape us, and ultimately expand our lives.

Bet Now

A question I'm often asked is "When should I bet?" and my answer is the same every time: **Bet now.** Don't wait until next week, and please do not wait until you feel comfortable. Bet in moments of change. Bet when you feel the nudge to activate your AQ. The nature of bets is that they are always uncertain, and if we wait until we're ready, we could be waiting for years. Stop delaying, overthinking, and holding back, and start now. Remember, you don't have to begin with a massive bet. I'm not suggesting you to sail across the Atlantic Ocean with a near stranger like I did. You can start small: Take a new route to work, try a different coffee shop, or cue up an unexpected podcast. If you want to start exercising, do it right now, with twenty jumping jacks and twenty squats. If you want to reorganize your home, set a firm, nonnegotiable deadline, and honor it no matter what.

What these examples have in common is immediacy. They demonstrate that action begins the moment you decide to move, even if the first step is simply setting a deadline or making a plan. With betting, your first step doesn't always have to be "doing." It can be thinking, drafting, or scheduling. What matters is inching yourself outside of your comfort zone—even if all you do is dip a toe in.

Remember: Bets are *movement*. They shift you from what's known and comfortable into the terrain of growth and possibility. As Newton's first law of motion says, objects in motion stay in motion, while objects at rest stay at rest. If you've been stuck in the Avoidant Stage for a while, you need to break that inertia—and the best time to do this is now. The earlier you begin, the easier it becomes, because the momentum of your bets will carry you forward.

There are two rules of thumb when it comes to betting. Here's the first: The more you want to avoid it, the more you need to do it. Resistance is a signal that you're stuck in the Avoidant Stage, and the only way out is through action.

Second: If something is still on your mind after twenty-four hours, act on it within forty-eight hours. This rule creates a time boundary—because sometimes urgency is what sparks our agility. Keep these two principles close. When fear creeps in and you hesitate to place a bet, let them propel you into action. In the spirit of betting before you feel fully ready, let's take a leap now. Write down one bet to make today—and take that first step as soon as you can.

The Fourth Try

At age fifty, James McMahon nearly stopped betting. After all, he had a stable career, mortgage payments, and two kids in college with two more at home. Financially and strategically, it was a nonideal time for big bets. On top of this, James had already placed—and lost—three significant bets when he started businesses that hadn't worked out. It would have been entirely understandable for him to stop. But instead, he chose to bet big for a fourth time and launch a new company.

It wasn't an easy bet either. In middle age, James signed up for long hours, immense pressure, and a highly uncertain future. Luckily, his wife Lauren was game to bet with him. Together, they decided to sell their home to free up capital for the startup, and the whole family moved into a much smaller apartment. Doubling down on their bet, his wife even joined the company, too. James and Lauren were twice the age of an average startup founder, but they didn't let that stop them. They bet hopefully, with conviction, and began building a complex software platform focused on climate risk analysis.

Four years later, James's bet paid off. The product was revolutionary, and an array of Fortune 500 clients signed six-figure deals. Soon after, acquirers came knocking. James sold the company, a move that allowed him to build his dream house, support Lauren in pursuing a new vocation, and gain the financial freedom to never work again. None of it would have happened if he hadn't made that fourth bet.

If you take away anything from James's story, let it be this: If there's something you want, you must be agile enough to bet *at least three times*. Your first bets will probably **not** work out—and that's okay. That's normal. So, you must keep going and betting until you reach your desired outcome. I wrote three different proposals before I found my first book editor. Tyler Perry made thirteen bets before his fourteenth play was a success. Brian Acton made and lost two bets, applying to and getting rejected from Twitter and Facebook, before he built WhatsApp. Even Vincent van Gogh had to keep betting. It took him nine hundred bets to get his first real sale.

The bets you don't win are in fact part of the magic. When James reflects back on his other companies, the ones that failed, he sees just how important they were to his history. "It's seemed like a very winding path," he said, "but I needed all of that, all the failures, the mistakes, all the learning, to be able to do this."

Just like James, we need many opportunities to sharpen our talents, stretch our skills, and grow our wisdom. No one is perfect out of the gate, and "overnight" successes come from years of unseen labor. We require time to refine our vision, test our assumptions, and fix what's not working. Every bet—whether it succeeds or not—builds our AQ. The real secret to winning is betting often. So, as you practice this new agility tool, don't take your first few bets personally.

A bet for me isn't necessarily a bet for you, and the same holds true across the Archetypes. A bold new hairstyle might be a huge bet for the Firefighter, but not risky at all for the avant-garde Astronaut. Or it might be easy for the Neurosurgeon to reach out to an old friend, while to the Novelist it seems like an impossible task. A bet for one is not a bet for all, and getting started requires some customization. For some fresh inspiration, let's explore betting ideas organized by Archetype. Remember, we bet as a means to increase AQ, so for maximum impact, focus on the bets that feel the most stretching, uncertain, or emotionally loaded.

How the Archetypes Play the Slots

If you're a Neurosurgeon, the most effective bets you can take serve one of two purposes: either to quicken your pace or to put you in new, unfamiliar situations. Let's tackle speed first. If you recall, the Neurosurgeon, who is diligent and detailed, can be challenged by **slowness,** and bets can be a great way to practice moving faster and offsetting that weakness. For example, if you're a Neurosurgeon, experiment with making one impulsive decision a week without doing any research, or set artificial deadlines for yourself that are 25 percent shorter than ideal. Push yourself to share works in progress before they're polished, or to deliberately choose the "good enough" option.

The second category of bets that are great for the Neurosurgeon involve deviating from an established lifestyle. This type of bet is important because the Neurosurgeon can get into a rut, with a strong preference for what they like and a closed mind for what they don't. That's why anything unfamiliar, unappealing, or unexciting is a great bet for the Neurosurgeon to take. Sign up for a project beyond your expertise or try a hobby outside of your wheelhouse. Or a bet can be as simple as letting others pick restaurants, hotels, or activities, even if they don't meet your expectations and standards.

If you're a Neurosurgeon and you're wondering whether or not to take a bet, ask yourself if it causes friction with your high bar for excellence, and if the answer is yes, then you should likely move forward.

For the Novelist, there's nothing more satisfying than when everything goes to plan—when the schedule is adhered to, the train shows up on time, and nothing unexpected arises. But since the point of making bets is to move us into the unfamiliar, the best bets that a Novelist can take are the ones they didn't initiate themselves. Anything outside the Novelist's carefully crafted vision becomes fertile ground for growing their AQ. For instance, if you're a Novelist at an awkward family gathering, a good bet to take is deciding not to leave early. You stay put and let the day unfold, even if it's against your plan. Or a bet could be accepting unsolicited help from a friend or gracefully adapting to last-minute changes. Letting go of control is one of the best bets you can take.

Because Novelists also grow when they become more forgiving of life's annoyances, finding the silver lining in unwanted hiccups and accepting disruptions with a smile are two good bets to take. You could also bet by increasing your tool kit for emotional overload: Experiment with mindfulness, begin keeping a journal, or practice taking deep breaths.

Use this rule of thumb if you're a Novelist wondering when you should bet: The exact moment you need to take a bet is when you're disgruntled, irritated, or feeling vexed. As you take actions different from your default, your AQ will grow.

Firefighters are already well-versed in taking big bets because betting is their greatest problem-solving strategy. They easily take leaps with incomplete information and dash off expertly into the murky unknown. However, most of those bets emerge from the same type of moment—last-minute, real-time, and spontaneous situations. If you're a Firefighter and you want to grow your AQ, you must also learn to bet in long-term, proactive scenarios.

Betting at work means making more time for foresight. Perhaps you set aside time for weekly strategic thinking, or you schedule a quarterly offsite for high-level planning. It also means thinking ahead about your own growth. Seek out mentors and advisors, and reach out not just for emergencies but even when nothing is on fire. Saying no and resisting the urge to personally handle every crisis are other ways to bet at work; try delegating, solving the underlying issue, or creating boundaries for your availability.

Firefighters must also take bets in their personal lives, shifting their attention from right now to further down the line. Plan a vacation six months in advance or formulate a five-year savings plan. Think ahead in interpersonal relationships, too: Arrange a reunion for your friends or create an annual birthday tradition. Both at work and at home, the best bets you can take all involve long-term thinking. You are certainly effective when living in the moment, but planning makes you even more agile.

Like the Firefighter, the Astronaut is fantastic at taking big bets. In fact, this Archetype bets so naturally that they might not even realize they're doing it. Risk-taking, audacity, and trying new things all fall within the Astronaut's comfort zone. However, this is only the case when they're following their passions. It's much less pleasant for them to bet when the subject matter bores them. If you are an Astronaut and you want to raise your AQ, put effort into the ordinary. To grow, take a moment to come down from floating in space and plant your feet on solid ground.

At home, this means making time for boring but productive responsibilities: setting a monthly financial budget or planning meals in advance, for instance. In relationships, bets entail doing the hard thing, not just the fun thing, like sharing your feedback with a loved one or setting a boundary and sticking to it. If you're an Astronaut and you're not sure how you should bet, ask yourself: "What's the *passionate* action I can take and what's the *practical* action I can take?" You raise your agility when you prioritize the practical, too.

To bet well at work means you need to do more than just follow your interests. You must get curious about the responsibilities that seem less thrilling, too. Take a co-worker to lunch who does something you have no clue about, or raise your hand for a project that will help fill in a gap. Step outside of your own space bubble. Take a break from your own vision and instead research competitors or read up on best practices. Of course, the Astronaut's gift is to see the big picture, but you'll get there much faster if you also bet on the details.

Better Together

Bets are always more fun when you can do them with someone else, so seek out a friend who knows their Archetype, too. Perhaps there are some bets you can embark on in tandem, or you can hold yourselves accountable with a regular check-in. If you make the right bet at a casino, a cash prize comes your way, so be sure to celebrate your AQ bets, too. Reward yourself, praise your friend, or head out on the town. Bets are exciting but hard work, and you deserve a little merrymaking for your efforts.

Anchors and Bets at Work

Bets and anchors exist in a pair, complementary forces that support and sustain each other. Anchors provide steadiness, keeping you grounded, while bets expand your horizon and propel you into new territory. If you want to raise your AQ, you need both—the security of anchors and the boldness of bets. One cannot thrive without the other. For instance, if you only spend time with your anchors, you become a creature of habit, stuck in your comfort zone. But if you bet repeatedly without the stability of anchors, you risk becoming disoriented and unmoored.

Nowhere is this more essential than in your professional life. Careers that stand the test of time rely on both anchors and bets. Anchors provide the stability to perform at your best, while betting creates possibilities for where your career can go. At any given time, you should be pursuing at least one significant bet—whether that means developing a new skill, expanding your network, or increasing your visibility. For years, improving my writing was my primary bet. Long before I sold my first book, I invested in the craft, and today it's become a defining part of my work. At the time same time, I invested in my anchors—my writing group, my office, and the routines that supported my efforts. Remember, the bigger the bet you're making, the more you'll need your anchors.

We'll explore career more explicitly in the third part of this book, but for now, I'll leave you with this: One of the most essential AQ skills you can build is learning how to **bet on your-self.** The world is unpredictable. It won't always move in your favor. But, like James McMahon, if you keep betting on yourself—again and again—you'll create enough opportunities for one of them to take you exactly where you're meant to go.

BETS EXERCISE

BET SMALL, OVER AND OVER

Choose three small bets from the list in figure 7 and make a plan to do them all this week.

CHAPTER 5

Class Is in Session

A whole lifetime is needed
to learn how to live.

—Seneca

"Nothing ever goes away until it has taught us what we need to know." This line is from Pema Chödrön's book *When Things Fall Apart: Heart Advice for Difficult Times,* which I think should be required reading for every student of AQ. Let me say it again— *"Nothing ever goes away until it has taught us what we need to know."* This means that when an incident of CHURN strikes your life, it will happen to you again and again until you extract the lesson that you are meant to take from it.

I have a client who struggled with her quarterly board meetings. There was one investor who was rude, derisive, and unsupportive. My client would dread these meetings and show up to them as a shell of herself—inarticulate, reserved, and easily pushed around by her board. This meek version of her made the investor who believed that my client was not bold enough even more aggressive, and it created a vicious cycle of bullying and fear for months.

After the third board meeting that followed this pattern, I shared the Pema Chödrön quote with my client and asked what it meant to her. She responded immediately. "I can't keep waiting for my investor's approval," she said. "I need to show up at this board meeting not caring what he thinks. I'm the one running this company. I'm the one who knows best." After my client absorbed this lesson, everything began to shift. Not only did the investor back off, but he became one of her most vocal advocates. The CHURN vanished, but only when my client learned to assert herself. The hardship had taught her what she needed to know.

I experienced my own version of this not long ago. My brother and I were on the phone, and he asked me to be nicer and more understanding toward our mother. I immediately disagreed. This is a familiar dynamic between us. He is a harmonizer—he wants everyone he loves to be peaceful and happy. I, on the other hand, am direct and believe in productive conflict. We are different in temperament and philosophy, and our disagreements typically spiral into argumentative back-and-forths. He makes his point, I make mine, again and again, until frustration builds and one of us abruptly ends the call.

But this time, I remembered Chödrön's words and realized it might be time for a different approach. Instead of standing my ground and launching into logical, carefully constructed arguments, I chose to listen. I asked him to share his thoughts, and when I really listened, something softened in me. I allowed myself to consider that maybe he was right. It was a small shift, but significant. We both felt it and since then we've both been listening to each other more. He's able to see my viewpoint, and I'm able to inhabit his, too. It was true for my client and her investor, and it was true for me and my brother: The CHURN in our lives disappears only when the lessons we must learn are complete.

This brings us to the third tool of agility, called **"Classroom," which treats every moment of your life, big or small, as an opportunity for learning.** When you embrace this mindset, you increase your AQ by easily acquiring whatever new lessons you might need to handle change, uncertainty, and the unknown. In my client's situation, she wasn't just going into a board meeting—it was her opportunity to build self-confidence. That conversation with my brother wasn't really about our mother. It was my chance to learn about empathy. When you practice the tool of **classroom,** everything in your life takes on the potential for learning. Walking the dog becomes an exploration of botany, and making dinner can be a chemistry lesson. Through the eyes of the eternal student, the world acquires more depth, more meaning, and endless opportunities for agility.

When Satya Nadella took over as CEO of Microsoft in 2014, it was a low-AQ organization. The stock price had been stagnant for a few years, and public sentiment viewed Microsoft as a bureaucratic beast that had missed out on big tech trends like mobile and social networking. There was endless work for Nadella to do. Some investors put pressure on Microsoft to break up or spin off into small divisions, and some pushed for more focus on enterprise products. While there were sweeping strategic decisions to make, Nadella understood what would drive even greater value—he needed to overhaul the culture by teaching Microsoft the agility tool of classroom. He styled this initiative as a shift from a "Know-It-All" culture to a "Learn-It-All" culture, understanding that corporate growth could only happen with agile employees.

Nadella got started on building an entirely new culture. He and his team created a comprehensive communication strategy to populate stories of what a Learn-It-All mindset looked like at work. Then he filled the hallways with supportive visuals and put quotes on coffee mugs. The mugs became so popular that people started collecting and trading them. Finally, Nadella rallied his executives and together they repeated this learning-oriented philosophy over and over again until it was ingrained in every employee. Of course, Nadella pushed new processes, like getting rid of stack ranking for employee reviews, but he knew that a learning mindset mattered most.

If you want to increase your AQ, you must do for yourself what Nadella did for Microsoft, shifting from a Know-It-All culture to a Learn-It-All culture. Don't worry, you don't need inspirational posters and mugs to get into the classroom mindset. You simply need to decide that your worth is not determined by what you know but rather, by how much you embrace what you don't know. I invite you to adopt this learning mindset right now and head back to school with me.

Figure 8: Know-It-Alls vs. Learn-It-Alls

Know-It-Alls	Learn-It-Alls
• I'm proud of my expertise.	• I'm excited by what I'm learning.
• I'm at the top of my game.	• I grow more than others.
• I stick with what works.	• I can always make it better.
• I want to be right.	• I want to be effective.
• I don't want to fail.	• There's no failure, just setbacks to learn from.
• It's embarrassing to say, "I don't know."	• I am confident enough to say, "I don't know."

Figure 8. Know-It-Alls and Learn-It-Alls are both ambitious and driven types; however, Know-It-Alls are rigid and motivated to preserve the status quo in which they are experts. Learn-It-Alls are agile because they place the importance of learning above all else.

Back to School

Let's start by stepping into the student's shoes. Imagine yourself back in the classroom, sitting behind a desk while a teacher drones on. What do you do to stay alert, focused, and engaged? What do you do to ensure that you're learning? Out of the many strategies you could employ, here are three we can use to boost a learning mindset. We call them **Agility Journal, A+ Questions,** and **Learning Goal.**

These three activities not only enrich the learning you do in the classroom but also support the learning you do in life. They will serve as our scaffolding as we build out our understanding of the classroom mindset.

AGILITY JOURNAL

Write it down, write it down, write it down. If you want to make sense and meaning of your existence, **you must write it down.** Without a record of what transpires in your life, everything you learn disappears. The days blend into weeks and years, and soon you look back and it all seems like a blur. Let's test this theory. Without consulting your phone or computer, what were you doing exactly one month ago? What did you eat for lunch? What did you learn? What was the best part of your day? Personally, I cannot say what the answers are when I ask myself these questions. I wouldn't know without consulting some artifact, like a photo, an email, or a calendar, and I imagine you're in the same boat.

So, if you want to be the best learner possible, you need a notebook in which you record what happens to you and why it matters. You also need to do this writing by hand. Handwriting is, of course, slower than typing. The average person types forty to fifty words per minute, three times faster than writing by hand. The slowness of handwriting is an asset, though, because it allows you to take your time to process what you've experienced and learned with second-order thinking. Because you can't take down every single word, you're forced to distill. To be agile, you must look for lessons, sift out the most important ones, then write them down by hand.

An easy way to start is to begin an Agility Journal and record just three observations each day, noting three simple things, including:

One way you were rigid—
These are moments when you were motivated by

status quo bias (page 3) or Ambiguity Aversion (page 88).

One way you were agile—
These are moments when you embraced change or uncertainty, or you tried something new.

Something you want to remember—
This could be a joke, a memory, an interaction, an insight, or an idea.

Try journaling for a week, and then, using your AQ, adjust. You can amend the questions based on what you want to remember and process each day. You can also experiment with the best time of day to write in your Agility Journal. Keep tweaking your process until it becomes something you look forward to doing each day.

I thrive on accountability, so a few friends and I have all devoted ourselves to keeping a five-year journal. This style of journal has a small space to write something down every day for five years, and it's organized so you can compare what you were doing on the same day of each year. For instance, every February 16 for five years exists on one page, and it allows you to easily notice how much you've learned and grown over time. I am motivated by the significance of keeping a steadfast record of my life over a long period, so I never skip a day.

A+ QUESTIONS

Who is the person, living or dead, you'd most want to share a meal with? Nelson Mandela, South Africa's first Black head of state and the leader in ending apartheid, is at the top of my list. I'd ask him what lessons he could teach the United States today. I'd want to know what it was like to grow up in a Xhosa village, and what advice he has for me as a parent. I'd ask him to tell me about the best day of his life.

Nelson Mandela was a Nobel Peace Prize winner and brilliant thinker with profound wisdom to impart, but even so, he made it his goal to listen, ask questions, and learn from others. A prime example of this were the meetings he'd host at his home, gathering the members of his cabinet around his dining table or his driveway for animated debate. During these meetings, it was said that Mandela was often the quietest, sitting back amid the energetic debate, listening, synthesizing, and absorbing the dialogue. When he did speak, he would be curious and inquisitive, wanting to explore others' ideas. Mandela, an immensely qualified and confident leader, did what many other leaders are afraid or unable to do—*he led from the back*, refraining from imparting his own wisdom to hear from his team first.

Nelson Mandela illustrates a fundamental truth about learning that seems counterintuitive at first blush: ***The most intelligent, wise, and seasoned individuals excel at asking questions.*** They don't make grand top-down pronouncements. They don't presume to possess the answer to everything. They are Learn-It-Alls—curious, open, and ever-evolving. No matter how much experience they've accumulated, there is always more to discover. Conversely, a hallmark of someone who is rigid, resistant to growth, or intellectually stagnant is the absence of inquiry. They assume they know and see no need to seek the input of others.

A Harvard Business School study by Alison Wood Brooks showed that **people who ask for advice from others are viewed as more competent, not less.** In other words, asking questions is not a sign of weakness but a mark of strength, so don't hold back from seeking guidance. Don't hesitate to acknowledge when something isn't clear. The ability to ask thoughtful questions is a defining trait of highly agile individuals, and there's no better time to start than today. To embody the classroom agility mindset, here are some questions and statements that you can weave into your daily conversations:

- Tell me more . . .

- What do you mean by that?

- What's your opinion on . . . ?

- What do you think I should do about . . . ?

- I don't understand what you mean by that. Can you clarify?

When you commit to becoming an agile Learn-It-All, you'll find that it's a more delightful path than you might expect. It's quite freeing to release yourself from the pressure to know everything. There's no need to be perfect; instead, you optimize for learning. Satya Nadella and Nelson Mandela both shared the same approach to knowledge: the wisest of us are perpetual students in the classroom of life, and especially skilled at asking good questions.

LEARNING GOAL

If you were to walk into a classroom and ask each student to share their goal for the course, you'd hear a wide range of answers.

Some might say they're fulfilling a math credit, others that they're hoping to make friends or build a well-rounded résumé and get into a top college. Regardless of the specifics, one thing is true—students are more motivated when they understand why they're in the room.

Take tennis legend Andre Agassi, for example. At age twenty-four, Agassi beat Pete Sampras, the world's top-ranked player, to win the Australian Open. This positioned Agassi to claim the number one spot for himself, so he committed to an intense new training plan. He bench-pressed twice his weight, used bespoke machines designed for his body, and often slept on his trainer's bench because he was too exhausted to drive home.

And then it happened. Agassi got the call from his manager that he was officially the best in the world, but instead of feeling happy, he felt lost. "I'm the number one tennis player on earth, and yet I feel empty," he wrote. "If being number one feels empty, unsatisfying, what's the point? Why not just retire?" The truth was, Agassi had never cared about being number one. It was simply what he thought he *should* want, and when he reached it, it left him more uncertain about his purpose than ever.

What followed was not pretty. Agassi started using crystal meth, his marriage unraveled, and within two short years, his ranking plummeted 140 spots. To rebuild himself, he had to discover true, authentic goals that mattered to him. For Agassi, this meant dedicating himself to charity, finding love again, and starting a family. These new goals, the ones he chose for himself, made a difference on the court and off. In 2003, at age thirty-three, he again became the number one tennis player in the world; and at the time, he was the oldest person to ever hold the title.

The takeaway is clear: We all need a goal to work toward at

any given time. Full AQ requires meaningful objectives, whether internal or external, simple or existential. My goal right now is to eliminate the "filler words" from my speech. I have a Post-it note on my computer to remind me to practice anytime I'm on a video call. One of my clients is focused on making his company profitable; another is working on becoming a strong manager. My child is learning to crawl backward and pinch me.

Your Learning Goal might be a skill to acquire, a project to complete, or a behavior to shift. It doesn't need to be as intense as overcoming a drug addiction or starting a charitable organization. What matters most is that it matters to you. When choosing your goal now, do as you would do in any classroom environment: Follow your curiosity, design with your nature in mind, and choose something that improves your daily life. A Learning Goal, no matter how small, brings clarity and purpose to your life.

Study Buddies

Now that you've turned your world into your classroom, what courses should you sign up for? Each of the Archetypes learns best in distinct ways so to make the most of your unique tendencies, here are some ideas for making the classroom agility tool more engaging and enjoyable.

If you're a **Neurosurgeon,** chances are you excelled in school, because you are **thorough, academic, and mastery oriented.** In fact, you may even have an advanced degree or certificate program under your belt. Your work ethic and high standards make formal learning second nature—which is great news for your agility, because the classroom tool will feel instinctive to you.

You already know how to learn, and you're good at it. As

you grow your AQ, you may want to employ other rigorous paths: mastering a new language, cooking technically complex recipes, or learning origami through intricate patterns. The most important note here is to have fun. Even when you're pushing yourself to the heights of mastery, let lightness accompany the learning.

The **Novelist,** by contrast, is **self-directed, expressive, and goal oriented.** They always need a *why* behind all that they do. If there isn't a larger purpose, they'll struggle to engage. As a Novelist myself, I would never take an art class just for fun or pick up a hobby for the sake of relaxation, but I do consistently devour business and self-improvement books that relate to my work or parenting journey.

If you're a Novelist, too, project-based learning with tangible outcomes will suit you best. Try vision boarding and mind mapping, attend skills-based weekend workshops, or explore personal development through structured journaling. It's important to remember that some of the best learning also happens through chance discovery, so as you map out your classroom strategy, challenge yourself to explore beyond your neatly mapped out plans.

Now let's consider the motivated **Firefighter,** who views the act of learning as a competitive sport. Their style is **fast, intense, and focused on winning.** That's why Firefighters do well with coaching from highly skilled experts. They want to be pushed forward with urgency and speed. If you're a Firefighter, you might be interested in taking classes from people at the top of their field, signing up for arduous challenges, or putting a tight deadline on anything you want to learn.

Firefighters learn in an explosive way—in sudden, speedy surges. To fully reap the benefits of your dedication and hard work, try to keep your learning going beyond that extreme initial phase, and find ways to incorporate and revisit your new tools even in the monotony of everyday life. To do this, it might be helpful to join a network of other learners, have an accountability partner, or keep a monthly cadence of meeting with a mentor.

Finally, we have the **Astronaut,** our **passionate, experimental, and innovative** learner. While the Neurosurgeon will adhere to the most challenging of recipes, the Astronaut throws the cookbook out the window. They're spontaneous seekers. They don't want to learn from pages or behind a desk. Instead, they want to experiment like a mad scientist in the laboratory of life.

If you're an Astronaut, you'll fare well by learning through invention challenges, experimenting with art projects, building prototypes, and testing your scientific hypotheses. Unlike the Novelist, you don't need a purpose, and unlike the Firefighter, you won't seek out a drill sergeant for a coach. You learn for learning's sake, not for a goal like the Novelist or a desire to win like the Firefighter.

To make the most of your passionate spirit, share your classroom endeavors with others. Gather your friends for creative collaboration or perhaps get up on the podium and teach what you know. Your excitement for learning is captivating, so share it as broadly as you can.

Class Dismissed

Now let's return to the quotation at the start of this chapter: *"Nothing ever goes away until it has taught us what we need to know."* There are two interpretations of this sentence. The first is daunting:

We're doomed to repeat painful CHURN until we solve life's riddles. But the second reading is more liberating—and it's the one we'll choose: Every challenge is an opportunity to learn. You don't need to be perfect. You don't have to become an expert, and you certainly don't need to be a Know-It-All. What matters more is to be a Learn-It-All, taking comfort in the fact that no matter what CHURN arises, you have the capacity to face it, learn from it, and adapt.

I'm often asked if age matters when it comes to AQ. Does an older person have lower AQ than someone who is younger? Growing your agility is akin to building your physical muscles. Yes, it is certainly easier to train to perform great feats of strength in your twenties, even if you're eating fast food, staying up late, and partying with your friends. Still, Sister Madonna Buder completed Ironman races into her eighties, and Yuichiro Miura climbed Mount Everest at age eighty. Agility is accessible no matter your age, but it does require focus, determination, and practice. Fortunately, when the whole world is your classroom, you never run out of material.

When I was growing up, the best students were the ones who got gold stars, earned good grades, and never broke the rules. The pursuit of AQ runs that paradigm through a paper shredder. The classrooms of our childhoods were orderly and unsurprising, while today's reality is spontaneous and erratic. The desks are upside down. The teachers change without warning. The knowledge that landed you an A might guarantee failure tomorrow. The high-AQ student takes in the chaos with a smile on his face. At least he knows he'll never be bored.

Classroom Exercise

THE AGILITY JOURNAL BEGINS

Decide how you will take notes, faithfully recording and processing the important learnings of your life in an Agility Journal. Complete your first entry today.

CHAPTER 6

The Discomfort Wave

Barn's burnt down—
now
I can see the moon.

—Mizuta Masahide

The physical experience of childbirth rates high on the McGill Pain Index, scoring close to 40 out of 50. This makes it significantly worse than chronic back pain, with a rating of 27, and nearly as bad as having a finger amputated, which scores 40. When I was five months pregnant, a friend, over a casual pizza dinner, described her unmedicated childbirth as "inside-out hell." I was terrified. Then, weeks later, another friend shared the opposite sentiment: "I had a completely pain-free birth experience." Yes, there was strong pressure, she admitted, but zero pain. Which is it, I wondered, heaven or hell?

I found out on a snowy day in January at home, one week past my due date. Light labor began in the morning, so gently, in fact, that I spent the day eating ice cream cake and watching *Grey's Anatomy* while pausing the TV to move through contractions. Things amped up around 3:00 P.M., but the experience was still so manageable that I assumed I was nowhere close to giving birth. I was wrong. At 5:14 P.M., my daughter made her way into the world with the midwife arriving just minutes beforehand to catch her.

I am not someone known for physical fortitude. I've cried because my face was too cold, and I often stop to rest and complain when carrying my groceries home. I attribute the ease of my birth experience not to physical vigor or mental toughness, but to **learning a new language.** For the nine months leading up to that moment, I chose the words I used to myself and with others carefully, swapping out the colloquialisms we know for a more peaceful and inviting set of words. Instead of *labor,* which connotes hardship and effort, I called it *birthing,* and I never once used the word *pain.* Rather, I described it as *sensation.* The word *contractions,* rigid and tight, shifted to *waves,* a word that speaks to an easy flow and rhythm. In the home stretch, I never told myself to *push.* Instead, I thought, "I'm just helping my baby make her way out."

This simple shift of language enabled me to perform one of my greatest feats of AQ—a pleasant, unmedicated home birth. I truly enjoyed myself, even though every aspect of CHURN was present in the process. There was **change,** profound change, to my body. There were **hiccups,** notably, movers who arrived at our home that day with a truck full of furniture. Dev and I were new to the process and filled with **uncertainty,** and there was **rupture** when our midwife arrived later than we had planned. Finally, there was **newness,** with the addition of our tiny new family member.

Neither one of my friends' descriptions of birth seemed right to me. One said it was awful, while the other said it was euphoric. My experience was more complicated. For me, birth was difficult *and* beautiful. Terrifying *and* exhilarating. Both befuddling *and* grounding at the same time. There was plenty of discomfort involved, but not in an unpleasant way. When I look back on that snowy, uncertain day, I consider it the most meaningful twelve hours of my life.

Perhaps, when you look back at your own life, you might find that you've experienced similar dualities that combine best and worst moments. After all, the harder the mountain is to climb, the better the view. When you accept this dichotomy of both unwanted and welcome in life, you come one step closer to mastering the final tool of the ABC's. We call it *discomfort,* and it means **accepting the challenging sensations in our lives, knowing that they signal growth.** This tool is about *learning to see discomfort as a good thing, a sign of your increasing AQ.* Understandably, this is the least popular of the agility tools. *Anchors* are safe and comforting, *bets* are fun adventures, and the *classroom* fills us with possibility. *Discomfort,* on the other hand, seems, well, uncomfortable. It's the pit in your stomach and your pounding heart. It feels like stress, anxiety, self-doubt, or even shame. I don't know many people who naturally enjoy discomfort, but if you want to raise your AQ and become more agile, it is essential that you not only make peace with discomfort but also welcome its presence as a harbinger of growth and agility.

The Pain of Monotony

In 1951, a Canadian psychologist named Donald Hebb had an enticing offer for students at McGill University. He'd pay them today's equivalent of $200 a day to sit in a room for a few weeks and do absolutely nothing while he and his team studied the impact of monotony and boredom on the human brain. The students jumped at the chance, imagining themselves catching up on sleep, thinking about schoolwork, and getting paid handsomely for it.

Their living quarters were spare but comfortable, with a simple bed and table in a small room. The students went down the hall for bathroom breaks, but for the most part, they stayed in the room. Anything that could cause variety in the environment was blocked out. White noise played in the background to minimize sound novelty, and the students wore gloves to dull their sense of touch. Even trips to the restroom were made as unstimulating as possible, with each student donning goggles to blur their vision. Hebb and his team planned for the study to last six weeks, expecting that "doing nothing" would be easy to maintain. But it wasn't. In less than a week, all but one student had quit.

The impact of this study on the participants was unsettling. After just a few days in a monotonous environment, the students simply could not think clearly. They failed elementary-level arithmetic tests and struggled with basic word association problems. On top of this, some participants hallucinated. One volunteer could see nothing but dogs. Another thought he heard a music box playing endlessly. A third felt a phantom electric shock each time he touched the doorknob.

This study took the experience of monotony to the extreme, but the findings apply to us all. As much as our status quo bias

drives us toward consistency, the truth is this: A life without varia-
tion results in us functioning at our worst. We need the new. We
need the novel. We need CHURN and the discomfort that comes
with anything new. Without it, we bore ourselves to the point of
cognitive malfunctioning.

The Delight of Discomfort

My friend Ssong's dad had an experience that most people would
consider not only discomforting but also unjust or even traumatic.
In South Korea, where Ssong was born, her father had been a
tech executive and an early pioneer in bringing e-commerce to
the country. He had it all—opportunity, excitement, and meaningful work—but when his business partner drained the corporate
bank accounts and disappeared, he lost everything he'd worked
for, and Ssong's family moved to New York City to start over
again.

Think about how uncomfortable it feels to travel to a new
country for a week. Now imagine moving there forever while simultaneously rebuilding your career from scratch. Most of us
would experience that kind of discomfort as defeat, but Ssong's
father was undeterred. He threw himself into his new identity as
a business owner in the Bronx—running a small shop that sold
clothing to local churchgoers who dressed to impress on Sundays. Over the years, he made a happy life for himself. He had
creative fulfillment, customers who loved his product, and enough
financial success to buy his dream home and put Ssong and her
brother through college. With Full AQ, he made a choice not to
become bitter about the end of his tech career, and he never
tried to re-create it. Instead, he fully embraced the new. "He

always talks about that low point as something he's grateful for," Ssong told me, "because he wouldn't have the life he has now without it."

It is no surprise that Ssong is like her father. She feels steady in experiences that most of us would find destabilizing. As a filmmaker, she regularly faces uncertainty and change: new locations, new crew members, and new stories to tell. She never knows if a job will take her to the Midwest, Norway, or Taiwan, or if she'll spend months editing in Vermont, waiting for the production schedule. Ssong once went undercover with her crew in rural Pakistan to get an interview at daybreak. She has filmed gurus and musical prodigies, and she has traveled to more than forty countries. Ssong learned her agility from her dad, who was her role model for embracing discomfort and CHURN with grace and optimism.

In fact, Ssong's earliest memory is one of agility. She was eighteen months old and brand-new to walking, tiny and unsteady on her feet. She recalls holding an egg in her family's kitchen. In her young life, she'd seen her parents cook breakfast countless times, but she'd never been trusted with this ingredient before. Then came the moment that still lives in her mind: Ssong dropped the egg, and it exploded across the floor—messy, raw, and unfixable. Even at that young age, she understood that something had gone wrong. A moment before, there had been no mess. Now there was a problem and she had caused it. She turned to her parents, expecting trouble, but instead her dad calmly cleaned up the broken shells. He wasn't angry. He wasn't flustered. He was unruffled by the CHURN, and this taught her something vital: Events are only as uncomfortable as we allow them to be.

Not all of us have had formative moments like Ssong's. In fact, in many ways, both overt and subconscious, we're told the opposite as children. When we jump and fall, we hear, *Be more careful next time.* We're only celebrated when we succeed, even if we put in the same effort but without the positive outcome. The message is this: *Your comfort zone is good! Discomfort is bad! Stay where it's safe and you can succeed!* If we didn't have parents like Ssong's who taught us to delight in discomfort, then we need to teach that to ourselves now as adults. As I did with my childbirth journey, let's start with language.

Deviation from Normal

From this moment on, you will define discomfort with these simple words: **Discomfort is deviation from normal.** That's it. It's not hardship, struggle, or an unwanted feeling that you need to get rid of. It's simply an indication that you're doing something different from what you usually do. It's just deviation from normal. It's the awkwardness of wiggling yourself onto a paddleboard for the first time. It's the self-consciousness of rewriting your bio. It's the nervous fluster of walking into a room full of strangers. Is this discomfort? Yes, of course it is, but it is also growth, and it's temporary. One day soon, on your third paddleboard excursion, or when those strangers become your friends, your discomfort will vanish.

With this definition of discomfort in mind, let's also explore the relationship between discomfort and the other ABC's of Agility. As you continue to sharpen and refine your AQ, you might notice that *B, C,* and *D* go hand in hand. When you take bets, this is inherently a *deviation from normal* as you try something different from what you've done before. Naturally, discomfort rides shotgun with every bet you take. The same applies to the classroom mindset, which is about seizing every moment as an opportunity to learn, and this learning is uncomfortable. It's going from one state of understanding to a deeper, more contextualized one, so this, too, is *deviation from normal*. Thus, if you're properly embracing the tool of classroom, you should be experiencing discomfort as you go, too.

This connection between bets, classroom, and discomfort creates a self-reinforcing positive loop. When you get better at any one agility tool, whether bets, classroom, or discomfort, any effort you make builds muscle in the others, too, and you grow your ability with all of them.

Discomfort Waves

Now let's return to where we began this chapter—on the floor of my den while I ate ice cream cake and watched *Grey's Anatomy*. My contractions were nothing like the dramatic depictions in movies: searing pain punctuated with explosions of sound. My own experience was radically different—not explosive, but rhythmic. Each contraction felt like a *wave*—a gradual buildup of discomfort that crested and then rolled away, bringing relief. I never feared or resented the contractions, because I recognized the pattern. The intensity would rise, then fall. In, then out. Predictable. Peaceful.

I have since transferred this language to my broader, non-child-birthing existence. What I formerly referred to as "highs and lows" of life are now simply *waves*, neither good nor bad, just a pattern of rolling in and rolling out. While a "high" or a "low" might last forever, a wave will always wash back out to sea no matter how hard it hits you in the moment. Language is everything when it comes to agility, and once you master the right reframes, you master this tool. It's not discomfort—it's a wave. And it's not a bad thing—you're just deviating from normal. We can always count on life to send us unrelenting CHURN. Luckily, now we know that nothing lasts forever, especially discomfort.

Figure 9: The Language of the Discomfort Wave

Low Agility Sounds Like	High Agility Sounds Like
• Discomfort means I'm failing. • I hate this feeling. • This feeling will never end. • Why is this happening *to* me? • I'm struggling.	• Discomfort means I'm growing. • I may not like it, but I accept it. • I know that it will get better with time. • Why is this happening *for* me? • I'm growing my AQ.

Figure 9. We've been socialized to see discomfort as a "bad thing," but great freedom and relief emerge when we understand that discomfort is a positive sign of increasing agility.

Now that we've reframed discomfort from something inherently bad to a simple wave, a deviation from normal, what does this mindset shift look like in practice? What are the decisions we make and the actions we take when we embody this agility tool?

Visualize the Crest

When you are at the lowest point of the discomfort wave and struggling to stay afloat, it can help to shift your focus to the crest, envisioning the easy, enjoyable part of the experience that is yet to come. You use your mind's eye to picture, in vivid detail, how it will feel to arrive on the other side.

In the midst of an anxious, sleepless night, put your focus on tomorrow: a new day and a chance to try again. In the depths of a tough work sprint, picture the perfection of the finished project. If you're in a rough patch with your partner, imagine how your love deepens at the end of this difficult moment.

Visualizing the crest was my secret weapon during labor. I'd slowly count down during the discomfort, while picturing the sweet relief that would soon come. This will work for any discomfort that comes your way. If you give your attention to the respite around the corner, you'll find it arrives faster than you expected.

Celebrate Yourself

It's hard to feel annoyed when you're triumphantly crossing the finish line of an endurance race. Your muscles might ache and your energy might be depleted, but your joy outweighs the discomfort. This same concept can also apply to your smaller daily struggles. You can vanquish the discomfort you feel when you celebrate yourself with ample enthusiasm. When you cheer yourself on, discomfort fades into the background.

What is celebration exactly? An effective celebration has two components: (1) self-appreciation and (2) a joyful activity. So, when you're in the thick of discomfort, ask yourself these two related questions: "Why am I proud of myself?" and "How can I enjoy myself right now?" Then make a real effort to celebrate yourself with vigor and enthusiasm. After a long day of writing and coaching, I write a short self-gratitude list, put on a nice outfit, and then take myself out for a smoothie. If I manage to exercise despite dragging my feet, I reward myself with a TV show while soaking in a warm bath. Smoothies and baths are my modes of celebration. What are yours? What small pleasures could mark your own moments of growth?

Whatever you choose, go big. Celebrate yourself boldly. You are doing something hard. And the more discomfort you navigate, the grander your celebration should be.

"I'm Growing My AQ"

I want to introduce you to a phrase that, when used on a daily basis, will cement your new relationship with discomfort. It's four simple words—"I'm growing my AQ"—and they're a new default response to any discomfort you face.

Imagine your kid catches the flu and the whole family is sick. You replace your old frustration with a reminder of progress. "I'm growing my AQ," you say, and you remember this is a chance to practice your agility. The power could go out, your boss could reprimand you, or your plane might be delayed. No matter how intense or surprising the discomfort, these four words, "I'm growing my AQ," are your salve, reminding you that discomfort improves your agility. To quote Archbishop Desmond Tutu, "Nothing beautiful in the end comes without a measure of some pain, some frustration, some suffering. This is the nature of things." Discomfort isn't optional. But growth and even enjoyment? That part is up to you.

Discomfort Exercise

CELEBRATE YOUR DISCOMFORT

What situation is causing discomfort in your life right now? In your Agility Journal, list three reasons you're proud of yourself for how you're handling it. Next, celebrate yourself and your AQ with a treat or reward.

Summary of Part 2:
Your CHURN, Your Choice

Now that you're familiar with the ABC's of Agility, let's play a game. I'll share three stories of individuals navigating the CHURN that accompanied their health challenges. Let's see if you can spot the ABC's—anchors, bets, classroom, or discomfort—each story brings to life.

Pete Wells

For more than a decade, if you walked into the back rooms of New York City's top restaurants, you'd find a picture of Pete Wells's face. *Alert management immediately if you see this person,* it might say underneath. Pete was *The New York Times*'s restaurant critic, a coveted job that required him to dine out five nights a week, devouring up to seven thousand calories in one sitting. As you might imagine, all that cream, butter, sugar, and alcohol had an effect on his body, but for most of his career, Pete dared not look too closely. "One thing we [restaurant critics] almost never bring up, though, is our health," he said. "We avoid mentioning weight the way actors avoid saying 'Macbeth.'"

One day, a visit to his doctor revealed issues with Pete's cholesterol, blood sugar, and hypertension. He heard the words *fatty liver disease, pre-diabetes,* and *metabolic syndrome.* He was technically, and unsurprisingly, obese. Instead of ignoring his body as he had for years, he finally decided to get educated about his health. Pete's job, this prestigious job, this job that was so entwined with his personality, had life-or-death downsides, and he gave himself the permission to explore another path. After surgery for an umbilical hernia, Pete took a break from his demanding restaurant schedule. Instead of gluttonous four-course meals, he ate simple salads and soups. His evenings, which had been busy and boisterous affairs, became quiet walks taken alone. Pete's recovery meant that he now had the space to pay attention, observe, and learn what his body needed. "At some point," Wells said of this departure from his status quo, "it occurred to me that I am not my job." He had acquired new information about his health, and he courageously let this knowledge change him. Pete scheduled time with his boss and officially quit what had once been his dream job.

Now that Pete is no longer a restaurant critic, his friends and acquaintances call him less. He stays home a lot more. His life is not nearly as exciting, dynamic, or glamorous as it once was, but even better, there is progress and growth. Pete's face may no longer hang in all the fanciest New York City restaurants, but it's a happier, healthier visage now.

I imagine we have all found ourselves in some version of Pete's shoes, needing to let go of some core part of who we are, something that defined us for a long time but no longer serves us now. It's such a hard task, and understandably, most of us avoid doing it for as long as we can. When we finally whip up the courage to change, it requires the willingness to learn, an openness to new information, and curiosity about the data in front of us.

Which of the Agility ABC's do you hear in Pete's story? Are you reminded of anchors, bets, classroom, or discomfort? I think of the third tool, *classroom,* which is about embracing the opportunity to learn and grow from every experience, whether we want to or not. Pete proactively took himself to the doctor and sought information about his health. When he got the data from the tests and blood work, he accepted it and allowed himself to be changed. To use the language of the classroom, Pete Wells asked questions and prioritized reflection. He learned a new body of knowledge, and with these insights graduated to a happier and healthier life.

Sarah Polley

It all started with a fire extinguisher at her local rec center. Writer, director, and actor Sarah Polley, fresh from a swim in the pool, hastily rummaged through the lost-and-found bin in search of a blow-dryer for her wet hair. She was in a rush, and as she flailed around, her shoulder accidentally dislodged the fire extinguisher above her, and the full weight of it landed on the left side of her head.

For the next three and a half years, Sarah struggled with post-concussion syndrome, which impacted every facet of her life. Normal activities she'd once done with ease, like shopping for groceries, taking her kids to school, or chatting with a friend, became unbearable. Even when Sarah avoided the things doctors told her to, like screens, gluten, dairy, and sunlight, she'd still get pounding migraines that forced her to lie in a dark room for hours. At the time of her accident, Sarah was adapting a film version of the book *Little Women* but had to give it up after the accident left her unable to work. That directing job then went to Greta Gerwig, who adapted her own version with Florence Pugh and Timothée Chalamet. It topped the box office and earned six Academy Award nominations.

During those years, Sarah saw doctor after doctor who all gave her roughly the same advice—don't push yourself too much. When you feel unwell, they said, back off and rest. They saw the migraines as a signal that her brain had maxed out its capacity, and she should avoid strenuous situations as much as possible. There was just one doctor, however, who believed the opposite. He told her to *run toward the danger.* He said Sarah would be fully cured in six weeks if she followed his method, but this meant doing all the things that she'd avoided for years because they triggered her nausea, fatigue, and headaches. Sarah asked the doctor how she should cope when the symptoms started, and his reply was aggressive. "Attack, attack, attack!" he said. "If I hear that you're having a nap, ever, I will yell at you."

Because nothing else had worked, Sarah tried out the new strategy. She chased loud noises and bright lights and dove into everything she feared. Sarah went to the grocery store and took care of her kids, and if any opportunity seemed like it might tire her out or provoke a migraine, she signed up for it. "I was in agony," she said. "Everything hurt." It was a curious, unfamiliar way of moving through the world, to proactively seek out that which unnerved her, but it worked. Six weeks in, just as the doctor predicted, Sarah was cured.

In the accident, Sarah had injured her vestibular system, the part of the brain that allows humans to interpret motion and busy environments, and for years, whenever Sarah avoided anything that activated this area, she prevented her brain from re-training itself. It was only by running toward the danger and seeking out painful stimuli that Sarah gave her brain the opportunity to strengthen itself and reverse the damage.

Even though her post-concussion syndrome days are behind her, Sarah still holds on to this mindset that saved her; in fact, it's become the foundational premise of her life. "I do all kinds of things now that I am terrified of," she said. She takes acting jobs that scare her, she wrote a memoir aptly called *Run Towards the Danger*, and just a couple of years post-recovery, Sarah adapted and directed her next film, *Women Talking*, which won her the Academy Award nominations she'd missed out on because of her accident.

Which agility tool does Sarah Polley embody? If you're thinking *D* for *discomfort*, you're right. For Sarah, healing, growth, and evolution only came when she sought out the stimuli and experiences that she most wanted to avoid. While few of us will ever be in her exact situation, with a yearslong brain injury, the insight here is relevant for us all—when we run toward the discomfort, we strengthen, we grow, and we ultimately find more ease.

Drew Bouton

Our last story is about Drew Bouton, a policy director from Washington state who was forty-five years old when he was diagnosed with stage four metastatic prostate cancer and given two years to live. Drew knew the odds were not in his favor. He understood that it would be a long and painful road of treatments and surgeries. Drew's doctors told him to prepare for the worst, but, despite his low chance of survival, he decided not to listen. Instead, Drew chose optimism. "From the very first day, I thought, maybe it will be different for me," he said.

With this mindset of hope, Drew signed up for clinical trials and experimental treatments and was one of the first people in the United States to receive a personalized immunotherapy called Provenge. Even when the symptoms and side effects were unknown, Drew took a gamble anyway. In his personal life, Drew did the same, too. Shortly after his diagnosis, he married his partner and together they adopted their daughter, whom they'd fostered since the start of his health battle. I imagine that most of us, given a prognosis like Drew's, would choose to have fewer responsibilities instead of more. We might quit our jobs, sell our cars, and spend as much time on the beach making bad decisions as possible. Why build your life if it will disappear anyway? What's remarkable about Drew is that he did the opposite. He set down roots. He started a family. He behaved as if he'd live forever, and in the process, it became a reality. It's been twenty-two years, and Drew is still alive, he's still married, and he's been by his daughter's side as she's grown into adulthood.

Which of the agility tools do you see in Drew's story? Maybe you're thinking of *anchors*. After all, Drew leaned into his partner and the child they fostered, deciding to commit even further to them during his time of huge upheaval. Or perhaps you think Drew embodies the spirit of *bets*, taking chances on experimental treatments and personal commitments, despite his inherently uncertain future. If you guessed either, you're right. In Drew's story, we see how intertwined these two tools are, with the grounding power of anchors serving as a complementary force for the riskiness of bets. Not only do anchors and bets balance each other out, but each one makes the other possible. Together, they are so powerful that they enable the impossible to happen, like Drew Bouton living two decades more and counting past his doctors' prognosis.

Pete, Sarah, and Drew—our exemplars of the ABC's are three very different individuals. While all of their stories involved huge, life-altering health issues, the way each faced this massive CHURN was unique. Each had a different strategy, their own interpretation of the agility tools.

Now I'll turn the spotlight around onto you. Which of these three stories felt most like what you would do? Would you, like Pete, seek out new information, data, and wisdom? Or would you run toward discomfort like Sarah, pushing into the unknown? Perhaps Drew is more your style, and you'd double-down on your anchors to get the energy for big bets.

Depending on your Archetype, you might find yourself drawn to some of these tools more than others. **Neurosurgeons** are experts at cultivating strong, supportive **anchors.** They have rich friendships, ties with places, and steady habits that they lean on.

Astronauts are great at taking **bets,** because their focus on the future means that they are less intimidated by unknown terrain. In fact, they may not even notice that they are taking bets because they are so used to operating in new situations.

Novelists, the researchers and planners of the group, do well with the **classroom** tool because they are comfortable and adept at accumulating information that will help them map out their future.

Finally, the **Firefighter** is our in-house expert in **discomfort.** They come alive in turbulence, so discomfort often doesn't even register with them. It's simply a normal part of daily life.

Your Archetype informs which of the ABC's come most naturally, but the situation may demand something different. Becoming high AQ means mastering all the tools regardless of your innate inclination. You can always take a moment to quickly run through the ABC's by asking yourself a few questions:

1. How can I get more steady, stable, and grounded? (**Anchors**)

2. What would I do if I knew everything would work out? (**Bets**)

3. What do I need to learn in this situation? (**Classroom**)

4. Can I reframe my perspective and accept this discomfort? (**Discomfort**)

Different situations will call for different combinations of the ABC's, so with the spirit of agility, experiment and try out new strategies. What you need today is not always what you will need tomorrow, so have fun, push yourself, and consider these tools life-saving medicine, because when you know how to use them, they truly are.

PART 3

What You Do

A man grows most tired
while standing still.

—Chinese proverb

Skills for the Future

Let's talk about what happened when a massive breakthrough in travel, equal parts thrilling and unnerving, sent shockwaves through the world. Thought leaders and scientists voiced concern that the force of the new technology, stronger than anything they'd encountered before, might cause serious harm to the human body. Predictions ranged from hearing loss and seizures to cerebral contusions. How could the government, people wondered, invest so much time, money, and manpower into something so unproven?

What was this disruptive innovation? Was it the multistage rocket, the nuclear submarine, or the supersonic jet? What's your guess? This alarming technology was none of them. It was the steam engine locomotive, also known as the train, an ancient mode of transportation we now know to be harmless. When we compare those first frightened fears of the train to the benign perception of it today, an important lesson emerges: We are truly ineffective at predicting what tomorrow brings. As writer, business educator, and "inventor of business management" Peter Drucker said, "The only thing we know about the future is that it is going to be different." We cannot and should not trust our first reactions to innovation, because more often than not, our emotional instincts are wrong.

I saw this up close during my time at a leading venture capital fund. For every company my firm evaluated, a memo was painstakingly prepared by a team of investors who'd graduated from Harvard and Stanford, extolling the virtues and predicting the pitfalls of some technology prophesied to change the world. I was swept up in the excitement, believing that these companies could indeed create the next Disney, reinvent higher education, or eradicate the opioid crisis.

This firm had an exceptional track record, and still, I learned that even the best-informed prediction is still just that: a guess. No matter how thorough at research, no one, not even the most successful investors on the planet, can predict the future with certainty. And if they can't, how can the rest of us? How do we navigate the waves of new technology and shifting industries? How do we know when a train is just a train, or if it is indeed a high-speed coffin?

Now let's turn toward your professional life. The chapters ahead offer future-facing tools to build a resilient career in a world that keeps changing. You'll meet real people and real companies grappling with the same hurdles as you—persistent change and massive uncertainty as they strive to create meaningful work. While our terrain is professional, you'll find these insights echo through your personal life as well. We begin with the first strategy: Durable Skills.

CHAPTER 7

Get Durable

Man is still the most
extraordinary computer of all.

—John F. Kennedy

Imagine your boss comes to you with a new, ambitious project that she wants you to run. It's the company's top priority, it's never been done before, and you're the only person who can make it happen. Your assignment? Train a monkey to recite Shakespeare while standing on a pedestal. You're not sure if it's feasible, but you accept the challenge, thrilled to work on the future of the business.

"So, what will you do first?" your boss asks. "Do you train the monkey, or do you build the pedestal?" Which one would you choose? How would you kick off this daunting, possibly undoable project?

Perhaps you build the pedestal first. There are many good reasons to start there. First off, you could get going right away, and while it might take some learning, it's guaranteed that you'd eventually construct the perfect pedestal and thus knock out a huge chunk of the project quickly. Choosing the pedestal gives you the fastest path to a tangible win.

The other route, to begin with the monkey, is more complex and speculative. You could be training that monkey for weeks, months, even years before you know if the end goal is even possible. It's the choice of most uncertainty. Starting with the monkey is signing up for a long road of hard work without any guarantee of success.

As unpleasant as that second route may be, the correct answer is to begin there, with the monkey. This question of monkey or pedestal is what Astro Teller, head of X, otherwise known as Google's "moonshot factory," uses to illustrate how the best innovation happens. A "moonshot," like when Apollo 11 landed humans on the face of the moon for the first time, is defined as an audacious and ambitious goal with potentially large-scale, transformative results. At X, this means that they pursue radical solutions to the world's most pressing problems, like monitoring ocean health, beaming the internet through lasers, and creating grid-scale energy storage. For all these projects, there's no guarantee that a solution is even possible, so, as Astro says, it's essential to tackle the hardest and most uncertain parts first. That's why you have to start with the monkey, because if you can't teach it to recite Shakespeare, then why even bother building the pedestal?

The Ladder and the Infinite Wall

This monkey versus pedestal analogy turns out to be excellent career advice, too. After all, our professional lives increasingly resemble moonshots—ambitious, unpredictable, and without a guaranteed road map—because we don't know what the future holds. This occupational uncertainty is terrifying, of course, but like a moonshot, it's also exhilarating. There is far less stability but far greater possibility. To unlock that possibility, you must be willing to step into the unknown and reject the traditional idea of a "steady career path."

Since the mid-1900s and the rise of big corporations and structured job hierarchies, the concept of "the career ladder" has permeated how we think about progress at work. You choose your ladder and commit to it, patiently climbing rung by rung, promotion by promotion, until you reach the top and retire at age sixty-five. I'm sure we can all agree that this model no longer reflects reality. Our professional lives are richer, more fluid, and more multidimensional than any ladder can account for. We aren't just climbing upward. We're also going sideways or diagonally, and sometimes floating free in space (especially if you're an Astronaut). Navigating one's career isn't climbing a ladder, but scaling a magic rock-climbing wall, with ever-changing holds and infinite routes.

Naturally, the skills needed to climb a ladder differ greatly from those needed to scale an unpredictable wall. The ladder requires commitment, dedication, and deep expertise in a single vertical. That mercurial wall, however, demands agility. When the future is uncertain, your best asset is to become a versatile, adaptive athlete—someone equipped to excel in any surprising scenario. In other words, it's time to de-emphasize *Technical Skills* and start building *Durable* ones.

Durable vs. Technical Skills

Constructing a pedestal is a Technical Skill because it's a specialized ability with a practical application. GAAP (generally accepted accounting principles), 3D modeling, and social media management are also Technical Skills because they're job-specific and tied to particular industries or technologies. Notice how they are not interchangeable. An accountant's core responsibilities would never include 3D modeling or Instagram optimization.

Durable Skills, by contrast, are highly transferable across roles, industries, and eras. They are broad human and cognitive abilities like creativity, communication, self-confidence, and of course agility. They're called *durable* because they withstand the test of time, remaining valuable through your entire career, regardless of how your job evolves or industry transforms. Unlike Technical Skills, which can become obsolete as the world changes, Durable Skills remain relevant—even indispensable—in any future.

According to Harvard's Digital Reskilling Lab, the average half-life of Technical Skills is now less than five years—and in some tech sectors it drops to two and a half. This means that every Technical Skill, no matter how essential it seems today, is on a countdown to irrelevance. Conversely, Durable Skills aren't displaced by technology. While AI will soon outperform humans in most Technical Skills, it is unlikely to outperform us in the areas that matter most—the human and Durable ones. Your Durable Skills don't just help you to hold on; they exponentially expand your options.

Figure 10: Durable vs. Technical Skills

Durable Skills	Technical Skills
• Agility • Clear communication • Creative expression • Confidence and self-advocacy • Learning aptitude • Hard work and resilience • Bias toward action • Empathy and active listening • Self-awareness • Critical thinking and problem-solving • Receiving feedback • Persuasion and influence • Relationship building	• Programming languages like Python and Rust • Proficiency in software like Adobe and AutoCAD • Data analysis using tools like SQL and R • Digital marketing • Operating specialized equipment like heavy machinery or medical imaging • Accounting and financial planning • Project management • Video and sound editing • Cybersecurity management

Figure 10. Durable Skills endure across time and circumstance because they are highly transferable across different jobs. Technical Skills are job-specific and tied to particular industries or technologies.

Knowing the difference in value between Technical and Durable Skills is the key to career success. In 1902, two brothers, Adolphe and Émile-Maurice Hermès, inherited a successful business making harnesses and saddles for horses from their father, and they renamed it Hermès Frères (Hermès Brothers).

In 1916, when the company still employed dozens of saddle craftsmen, Émile-Maurice traveled to the United States, where he met with Henry Ford, the purveyor of the carriage-killing automobile, and understood that this "mechanical horse" would take over the world, and saddle making would become a defunct Technical Skill. Émile-Maurice's brother, Adolphe, understood the inevitability of this future, too. Three years later, after a steep decline in the sales of horse harnesses and equipment, Adolphe left Hermès, believing its demise was imminent, and allowed his brother to buy out his shares.

Since then, Hermès has done the opposite of what Adolphe predicted. The company is one of the highest-valued luxury brands, with a market cap of €247 billion. This happened because Émile-Maurice knew that the value of the company was far greater than its *Technical Skill* of saddle making. He understood that Hermès still possessed the *Durable Skills* of innovation, design quality, and branding.

When Émile-Maurice visited the Ford factories, instead of leading with his identity as a saddle maker and treating the new automobiles with fear and skepticism, he allowed himself to be open and interested in the new technology. Fastening the cloth top of a car, he spotted something he'd never seen before—a zipper. He jumped on this new technology, secured the patent, and obtained the exclusive rights to use it on leather goods and clothing in France. Seamlessly shifting from saddle making to clothing design, Hermès was the first luxury brand to use the zipper on high-end items, even displaying one on a golf jacket for the Prince of Wales in 1923. Under the guidance of Émile-Maurice, Hermès not only stayed relevant but became an innovator in European design.

Two brothers. Two different reactions. Adolphe Hermès saw the extinction of saddle making as proof that the company was doomed. Émile-Maurice, on the other hand, knew that Hermès was much more than just its Technical Skills. He focused on its Durable Skills and retrained to the context of the moment to create a brand that even now, a century later, is still a market leader. This hundred-year lesson is more relevant today than ever: When we overidentify with our own Technical Skills, we lose sight of the real, durable value we have to offer.

I see this all the time with young startup founders who are in the upper echelon of computer science skills. They code beautifully, but they flounder as CEOs because they haven't developed the Durable Skills to motivate a team. I also see friends who invested in graduate programs like accounting, law, architecture, and data science become stuck, afraid to pivot from work they don't enjoy. They've invested so much into these Technical Skills that they see them as their primary advantage. *I'm no one without this skill*, they think. To understand ourselves accurately, we must think less like Adolphe and more like Émile-Maurice, acknowledging that we have far more to offer than just our Technical Skills.

This may seem counterintuitive for a book on agility that was written at a time of breakneck tech innovation, but I want to encourage you to pause, slow down, and take your time to develop your *Durable Skills*. This is not to say that Technical Skills aren't important. We of course need to constantly teach ourselves the newest software programs, tech tools, and specializations. We all fear that new technology will take our jobs, but it is in fact the people who know how to use it who are our competition. So, we should be learning new Technical Skills all the time. However,

Durable Skills are primary. After all, your Durable Skills are what enable you to excel at learning new Technical Skills. For example, before you can teach yourself how to edit photos using AI, you need to have a few Durable Skills, including:

1. The **self-awareness** that you have a skills gap

2. The **learning aptitude** to teach yourself something new

3. The **work ethic and resilience** to keep trying, even when you struggle

4. The **critical thinking** to come up with novel ways of applying the new skills to your work

If you're still confused about the difference between Durable and Technical Skills, a helpful framing is to ask yourself what AI can do right now. For instance, AI can analyze documents, code websites, perform complex math, and write summaries and instructional guides. Those are all Technical Skills that will inevitably become less important for humans to do.

But can AI build long-term relationships, detect subtle emotional cues, resolve conflicts, arrive at new insights, make intuitive creative leaps, or lead a team through change? These are Durable Skills, because we humans innately outperform technology in these departments.

Honing your Durable Skills means reading books about personal development, management, and leadership. It's about improving your ability to communicate in person, in emails, in memos, and via slides. Grow your Durable Skills through a regular schedule of continual learning: Don't watch YouTube videos just for the exact technical knowledge you need right now, but commit instead to a lifelong mission of becoming a high-AQ, all-terrain athlete equipped to scale the infinite wall of work.

The most advanced AIs are large language models (LLMs) that have been trained on nearly all the information available to them in the world. If we want to remain relevant no matter how technology shifts, we must think of ourselves as LLMs, too, and fill our own training data with distinctly human experiences like building relationships, deepening self-awareness, meditation, and creative expression. We let AI be the worker because it will always beat us in that arena. Instead, we hone our rightful human potential of genius.

When we learn Technical Skills, we prepare ourselves for a specific moment in time and a particular situation, which will inevitably become irrelevant. With Durable Skills, we become context-agnostic, able to contend with any shifts in technology, culture, or geopolitics, regardless of how jarring. By cultivating our Durable Skills, we become timeless, unique, and invincible.

Durable Archetypes

If you're a **Neurosurgeon** who wants to increase your durability, your focus should be on one thing: **speed.** You've already mastered diligence, thoughtfulness, and a sky-high standard of excellence, but to become durable in today's changing workplace, you need to move faster. This means choosing action over imperfection and learning to make decisions with incomplete information. A useful tactic is to set "speed deadlines" that are earlier than you feel comfortable with. These deadlines will push you to pivot when in the past you might have stayed the course.

Ask yourself often: *How can I run faster and take bigger leaps of faith? How can I stretch my threshold for discomfort?* At work, this might look like raising your hand for unproven projects or collaborating more with people you don't know well or don't like. If you're actively trying to improve a Technical Skill like financial modeling or photo editing, put it into practice far sooner and far more often than makes you feel confident. Your goal is to get in motion—faster, looser, more adaptive.

For **Novelists,** your work is to become more **open-minded** to the ideas, perspectives, and plans of others, even if they conflict with your own. Remember, the Novelist's gift is writing their own story. They know what they want and have a plan to get there, and while this sense of personal conviction is commendable, it doesn't leave much room for the viewpoints of others.

If you are a Novelist, ask yourself these two questions at work: *How can I learn and grow from others? How can I become more flexible?* In practice, this might look like seeking out feedback, being less skeptical of others' perspectives, or making group collaboration a priority. As you develop these skills, take a cue from the Neurosurgeons you know. Stay with it. Keep showing up when plans change. It might turn out better than you expected.

Our brave **Firefighters,** meanwhile, must cultivate **reflection** if they want to become durable. Remember, Firefighters thrive in the chaos and pressure of immediate challenges, and while this is a great strength, to increase their overall aptitude, they must learn to do the opposite—slow down and make space for proactive planning. Firefighters become more durable when they learn to implement preventive measures.

If you are a Firefighter, ask yourself these two questions: *What important (but not urgent) issue am I currently neglecting? Am I moving too fast for self-awareness and reflection?* To give these questions the space they deserve, build habits and structure into your routines, including making time for daily reflection. Firefighters, remember—your durability spikes when you realize that slow work is good work, too.

Finally, let's explore how the **Astronauts** among us can foster durability. To develop your Durable Skills at work, let **expertise** be your North Star. If you're an Astronaut, you do well because your passion and curiosity pull you into an array of interests. While being a generalist is certainly beneficial for AQ, growth occurs by optimizing for depth over breadth. Instead of embarking on projects through trial and error, try your best to prioritize methodology and preparation.

To build your durability, ask yourself these two questions: *How can I deepen my knowledge on this topic? How can I learn from experts, structured courses, and books?* As you explore these two prompts, prioritize focus. Choose one area at most to improve at any given time. Then stick to it for longer than you typically would. At your job, sign up for continuing education, seek out mentors, and devour anything you can about the most important work on your plate. As an Astronaut, you'll become more durable when you emphasize mastery.

Let the durable goals—**speed, open-mindedness, reflection, and expertise**—inspire the Technical Skills you learn, too. When you look at individuals with long, impactful careers, you'll see that yes, they have technical skills in spades, but also, they don't cling to them. They are learned, applied, and replaced with new technical skills when the world shifts. Their identity is not attached to what they know, but rather to how they grow.

The Party Promoter Pipeline

Let's take a moment to explore a few career paths and the Technical Skills needed to be good at each one:

1. **Party promoter**—Graphic design for marketing materials, accounting, event production, ticketing operations, venue logistics

2. **Artist management for musicians**—Contract negotiation, tour budgeting, royalty distributions, partnerships dealmaking, music distribution

3. **Crypto startup founder**—Blockchain protocols, fundraising, interviewing and hiring engineers, product strategy, user experience (UX) design, people management

4. **Product manager at a big tech company**—Data analysis, sprint planning and execution, product analytics, KPI (key performance indicator) tracking, wireframing and prototyping, writing product requirement documents

5. **Venture capital investor**—Advanced financial modeling, writing investment memos, technical due diligence, understanding of business models, unit economics calculation

Notice how distinct the Technical Skills are in each of these roles, even within similar industries. Now ask yourself this: What would you do if you had to start one of these jobs tomorrow? Then, what if you had to switch to the next, just as you'd hit your stride? I know someone who's done exactly that—and not just survived the transitions, but thrived in each one. Over the course of ten years, he went from throwing parties in Montreal to joining one of the best VC firms in the world before leaving to start his own fund.

You might be wondering how this person managed such big career shifts. Did he go back to school to change industries? Did he teach himself how to code? Did he have personal connections who helped him get his foot in the door? The answer to all these questions is no. His name is Jesse Walden, and not only did he have a successful, self-made career in the music industry, managing top artists like Solange and Blood Orange, but in a complete industry pivot, he moved to tech, started his own company, sold it to Spotify, then joined Andreessen Horowitz's crypto investment fund. A few years later, with an infant at home, he started his own fund. He has architected incredible career progressions based on the strengths of his Durable Skills.

When Jesse becomes interested in something, whether concert promoting, artist management, or the blockchain, he leans on his well-developed Durable Skill of **following curiosity** to become an expert on the topic. His written and verbal **communication** is another standout Durable Skill. In fact, when Jesse was still managing musicians and knew no one in the tech industry, he left a comment on a prominent VC's blog, written with insight and depth, and the investor responded, impressed by Jesse's observations. That small interaction enabled him, an outsider, to raise the funds needed to start his own company. The rest is history. When you track Jesse's story, you can see how his Technical Skills played their part, but the main driver that propelled him from opportunity to opportunity was his Durable Skills.

Learning over Outcomes

The irony is this: In order to develop Durable Skills, we have to stop caring so much about short-term achievement. This will be hard for anyone who is results oriented, who wants to win, be productive, and slash through their to-do list. (I'm especially thinking about all the impact-motivated Firefighters out there.) Cultivating Durable Skills requires a perspective flip. When you sit down to plan your day (or your career), you ask yourself, "What can I learn?" instead of "What can I accomplish?" This mindset of prioritizing *learning over outcomes* is what allows your Durable Skills to grow.

For instance, I wrote a draft of a chapter and read it to a friend. She cheered me on with copious amounts of praise. I could have left it at that, satisfied with her enthusiasm, but instead I pushed for constructive critique, determined to make the chapter better. In this small moment, I cultivated my durable skill of **receiving feedback.**

In a more complex scenario a client recently asked me to facilitate a workshop and left the topic entirely up to me. I could have chosen a familiar subject that I've delivered dozens of times, but I opted for something brand-new, something I don't yet know well. It will take me at least ten extra hours to prepare, but it's worth it. I'm investing in my **learning aptitude.**

You'll find that you, too, have ample opportunities to prioritize **learning over outcomes** and increase your **Durable Skills.** When it comes to advancing your learning, if you have an option to progress faster or slower, choose slower. Let me say this clearly: Slow is good. Deep learning—the kind that sticks and shapes you—takes time.

The Stages and Archetypes

Developing Durable Skills is essential for moving from the Avoidant Stage to the Fighting Stage. As you may remember, the Avoidant Stage represents the lowest expression of agility and is characterized as **rigid, withdrawn, and stuck** (see figure 5, page 58). In this stage, we dodge the CHURN in our lives, not because we're lazy or unaware, but because we lack the confidence to confront it. We feel powerless to make an impact, so we don't even try. This is where Durable Skills come in. They build confidence. They help us trust ourselves. They instill in us the knowledge that we can thrive, no matter the context or situation. This shift from powerlessness to proactiveness is the defining movement from the Avoidant Stage to the Fighting Stage.

Some Archetypes take to Durable Skills more naturally than others. Neurosurgeons and Novelists are always working on theirs. It's second nature for them to look inward and seek out ways to improve. Firefighters, on the other hand, who are wired for speed and action, are better at "just-in-time learning" than the slow cultivation required for Durable Skills. For Astronauts, the key variable is passion when it comes to evolving their Durable Skills. If they're deeply interested in a topic, they'll go all in, but they may need a push to develop skills that don't excite them.

Regardless of our type, we all have the same expansive ability to hone our Durable Skills. Now that you've learned how important they are, I'll ask you to reconsider the challenge of teaching a monkey to recite Shakespeare while standing on a pedestal.

Knowing what you know now, where would you start? Maybe you'd peruse *Hamlet*, contact an animal expert, or try to win over the monkey's trust with a banana. Or perhaps you'd practice with a parrot, a robot, or even yourself as a test subject. Whatever your tack, your success will rely on your Durable Skills like creativity, problem-solving, and resilience. They'll hold no matter what the monkey does or what technology threatens your livelihood, and like Émile-Maurice Hermès or Jesse Walden, you'll be ready for change with AQ on your side.

With a better understanding of high-AQ skills, we'll turn to how a high-AQ team functions in the midst of workplace CHURN.

CHAPTER 8

The High-AQ Team

A single arrow is easily broken,
but not ten in a bundle.

—Japanese proverb

I have a confession to make. I've had seven bosses in my adult professional life, and I've clashed with every one of them on a regular basis. I've fought with my managers about everything from high-level strategy down to the layout of a single Keynote slide. And yet, despite conflict, I truly enjoyed working for all of them (except for one who shall remain unnamed). With those six leaders, I evolved as a person, and together we produced results

I'm immensely proud of. Through the lens of AQ, I now see that both the conflicts *and* the successes with my bosses stemmed from the same source—their personalities were so different from mine, and while this often created friction, it also supercharged our shared ability.

Of those six great bosses, three were Neurosurgeons, two were Astronauts, and one was a Firefighter. From the Neurosurgeons, I learned about thoughtfulness, excellence, and how to play the long game. The Astronauts taught me how to think bigger and speak bolder. And of course, my Firefighter boss taught me not to sweat the small stuff—to stay cool in a crisis and focus only on what matters. I am who I am today because I had a front-row seat to these exceptional minds that expanded my own. This is true not just for me, but for all high-functioning teams— a variety of Archetypes makes for a variety of talents.

Consider the drawer of utensils that sits near your kitchen stove. It's not very helpful if all you have is a spatula. Sure, you can make an omelet, flip pancakes, or even sauté some veggies, but you'll struggle to cook well consistently without a knife, a grater, a ladle, and for quick meals, a can opener. Similarly, high-AQ teams work best when they have Astronauts, Firefighters, Neurosurgeons, and Novelists, or at least people who can flex into these types.

If you have a **Neurosurgeon** on your team, maximize their strengths by assigning them long-term, high-stakes projects that demand rigor. I regularly remind my clients that running a business requires knowing the difference between a "glass ball," something that cannot be dropped, and a "rubber ball," which can bounce back without damage. The "glass ball" work should go to the Neurosurgeon, who will guard it with care.

With a gift for Proactive Change, **Novelists** are ideal for launching projects, exploring new technology, or reimagining out-dated systems. Most of our work requires either a microscope (detailed, analytical, and short-range activities) or a telescope (big-picture, future-focused vision). It's best to delegate telescope tasks to a Novelist.

Firefighters are naturally drawn to urgency, so let them lead on projects with a tight or even unrealistic deadline. They won't feel intimidated as the other Archetypes might. Another talent of theirs is unorthodox problem-solving, so hand them the messy and complex challenges that overwhelm others.

Then there's the **Astronaut**—bold, fast, and unafraid of CHURN. Skilled at both Proactive and Reactive Change, Astro-nauts bring fearlessness to moments of transformation. When it's time for a moonshot, they're the ones to call. They won't be daunted.

Figure 11: Archetypes on a Team

	Ideal Contribution
Neurosurgeon	High-stakes, long-term "glass ball" projects
Novelist	New technology, innovation, and storytelling
Firefighter	Unwieldy problems and high-intensity situations
Astronaut	Moonshots, uncharted or experimental work

Figure 11. A high-AQ team has an array of Archetypes who are properly deployed against work that complements their talents.

Notice how each Archetype serves a distinct purpose. Mas-sive "glass ball" projects go to the Neurosurgeon, while impos-sible situations are the domain of the Firefighter. Perhaps the

Novelist works on goal setting, and the Astronaut handles change management with daring. When it comes to building a high-AQ team, homogeneity is out. The teams who thrive in the face of CHURN are the ones that draw on a rich mix of personalities, perspectives, and strengths.

The Stages at Work

Whenever you blend opposites— introverts and extroverts, task-oriented and relationship-oriented thinkers, and detail lovers and big-picture dreamers—it's a setup for friction, tension, and conflict, especially in the lower Stages of AQ.

Imagine a team stuck in the Avoidant Stage of AQ, where each person clings tightly to their own viewpoint. The Novelist doesn't understand why the Neurosurgeon obsesses over data quality, and the Neurosurgeon is baffled by the Novelist's cavalier attitude. Remember, the Avoidant Stage is **rigid, withdrawn, and stuck,** with a motto of *"Resist it."* Teams at this Stage fail to use the tools at their disposal. The spatula thinks every task calls for flipping, while the can opener insists that twisting is the only way. They can't fix problems or create solutions because they can't even agree on where to begin.

Teams at the Fighting Stage fare a bit better. They're more productive, but there is a similar strife and frustration. As you'll recall, the Fighting Stage is **critical, negative, and energy-wasting,** and the teams in this stage battle it out. They argue. They vent. They talk behind their teammates' backs. Yes, with *"Deal with it"* as their motto, they work hard toward a shared goal, but their default is to criticize and assume that their teammates have negative intentions. Then, when the work doesn't go according to plan, they blame one another. Imagine the grater, ladle, and spatula all jockeying for the same job, then pointing fingers (or is it handles?) when dinner doesn't get made.

Of course, the goal is the Full AQ Stage, where agility is fully activated. The motto of Full AQ is *"**Embrace it,**"* and team members do exactly that. They don't argue to win—rather, they collaborate to understand. There's no blame or defensiveness, only shared ownership. The mindset is **logical, unemotional, and thankful.** At the Full AQ Stage, every team member shines, receiving the respect, recognition, and trust they deserve.

The formula for a high-AQ team is not complicated. You simply need two crucial ingredients: (1) a variety of Archetypes on your team and (2) consistent Full AQ behavior. Easier said than done, you might be thinking. After all, we can't force the people around us to adopt a Full AQ mindset. You're right, but you can control something critical, and that something is *you.* Even if your entire team is stuck at the Avoidant Stage or the Fighting Stage, if you continue to show up every day with high AQ, you become a role model and blueprint for what's possible.

One of my clients once hired what he believed to be his dream executive team. They were passionate, smart, and determined, and together, their efforts led to a banner year of sales and an equally impressive round of financing. On the heels of these achievements, my client expected his team's mood to be celebratory, but instead it was anxious. *What if we can't keep up this pace?* they wondered. *What if our new investors push us in the wrong direction? The whole company, including us, is burnt out,* they said. Their pessimism blindsided him. He had scraped and toiled for this moment, and his dream team responded with anxious negativity.

Weeks passed and the tension didn't ease. At their next leadership meeting, my client finally said what was on his mind. He called out the negativity and asked why no one seemed excited. Silence. There were glum faces all around the table, until finally, the COO spoke up. "It's hard for us to get excited when you seem so anxious," she said. "In fact, the other day I asked you if you were happy and you said, '*We'll see what happens—I'm mostly overwhelmed.*'" The other executives nodded in assent while my client thought back and saw that his team was right. He'd expected Full AQ from his team, while showing up himself in the Fighting Stage. From then on, he was determined to set a better example, and within days, the team followed suit.

For better or worse, your AQ (or lack thereof) influences everyone around you, so you may as well use it to lead. If a colleague is stuck in the Avoidant Stage, ducking reality and not confronting the issues, you could take them for coffee and logically point out new options. Or, if a teammate comes at you from the Fighting Stage with sharp reactive energy, don't escalate. Instead, elevate the conversation with the thankful mindset of Full AQ and express gratitude for their insights. We all know that the people around us matter, but your own AQ matters more. When you embody the calm, clear, and grateful mindset of Full AQ, your team becomes a force nothing can rattle.

CHAPTER 9

The High-AQ Manager

In the universe great acts are
made up of small deeds.

—Lao-tzu

Before Nike was Nike, it was a company called Blue Ribbon Sports. For seven years, they were a homegrown little business that didn't make a single Nike product. In fact, they didn't make any products at all. They were the U.S. distributor for Onitsuka, a Japanese shoe brand.

It started as a passion project for the founder, Phil Knight, who sold these shoes he so loved from the trunk of his car. By year seven, it had thirty employees and millions in annual revenue, and Phil was finally able to give himself a raise. Now let's briefly pause this story. After studying agility for the past eight chapters, can you venture a guess as to what happened next? If you guessed big CHURN—you're right! Just as the company had found its footing, it fell off a cliff, and it was Phil's job to break the bad news to his team.

"Yesterday, our main supplier, Onitsuka, cut us off," he told his employees. "We've threatened to sue them for damages, and of course they've threatened to file a lawsuit of their own," he said. "We're completely on our own. We're set adrift." He then explained there was a *possible* life raft, a shoe concept of their very own, but there were issues with production that might not be fixed in time to save the company.

In that moment, what the Blue Ribbon Sports team wanted more than anything was *certainty*. They craved a guarantee that everything would be okay. But that was impossible, so instead Phil gave them what he could. He offered them AQ. "This is the moment we've been waiting for," he said. "Let's not look at this as a crisis. Let's look at this as our liberation."

The Full AQ Stage is defined by three notable qualities: It is *logical, unemotional, and thankful*. Did you notice how Phil's delivery had all three in spades? Did you see how he rallied his team to take a **bet**? Did you spot his willingness to sit in **discomfort**?

If you feel inspired by Phil Knight and his high-AQ leadership, this chapter is for you. It's an action plan for managers—those generous souls who reach beyond their own careers to shepherd, support, and invest in the work of others. Most of this chapter will *not* be about big CHURN like the Blue Ribbon Sports/Nike pivot. In fact, the focus here is on the tactical responsibilities of people management, because the best managers know that mastery lives in the details. Let's start with how to interview and hire high-AQ people for your team.

High-AQ Applicants

As someone who has interviewed thousands of people in my career, I'll tell you this: Never trust a résumé when it comes to AQ. Some of the most rigid candidates look the best on paper, with prestigious degrees and golden career paths. It's tempting to rush these individuals through the interview process, especially if you think you want someone "perfect." But remember, you're not hiring for "perfect." You are hiring for agility, and agility rarely travels in a straight line. It lives in zigzags, detours, and bold decisions, so most high AQ people have backgrounds that raise questions or challenge linear expectations.

I'm not saying you should reject every "good on paper" candidate outright. If someone looks talented, you should certainly interview them, but you must have a rigorous interview process that thoroughly vets AQ, and thorough vetting begins with the job description.

To hire with AQ in mind, your job description should read like an acquired taste. In fact, it's *ideal* if some candidates are turned off by it. You want to filter out the low-AQ applicants, so explicitly state that you are hiring for AQ and that you need someone who embraces *change, uncertainty, and the unknown*. Your job description should also mention the **Durable Skills** that you need in the role, in tandem with any requisite Technical Skills. For extra clarity, use the cover letter and as a mini AQ assessment. Here are some ideas:

- "In your cover letter, choose an attribute or skill in the job description that you do **not** have, and explain what you would do to acquire it quickly."

- "Describe the most unexpected, surprising career decision you made, and explain your logic and motivation for making it."

Agile Interviewing

I love designing interview processes. What better challenge than trying to glimpse a person's essence in a single conversation? My ethos for interviewing is to be direct. Of course you need to sell the company, but you also must be blunt about what you want in the role. This is why, in the first official interview, you need to talk about AQ.

You could do this by asking the candidate about their professional moments of CHURN. What happened and how did they handle it? Inquire about times they've taken bets, learned through the skills of the classroom, and persevered through discomfort. When it's your turn to describe the role, emphasize the agile, ever-changing nature of the work. As you go, pay attention to the candidate's reaction. Do they seem enlivened or hesitant? Your work is to be a sleuth, searching for signals of AQ or rigidity.

Finally, I'm a proponent of "project" interviews that simulate the true responsibilities of the position. (These projects shouldn't be lengthy, unless you plan to pay candidates for their time.) Since you're assessing AQ, it helps if the project has ambiguity. There shouldn't be a black-and-white "right answer," and don't overexplain the ideal output. High-AQ candidates will enjoy wrestling with the unknown. Every project prompt should be designed specifically for the role, but here are some general ideas:

- Send the candidate an article or a case study and ask them to write five hundred words explaining what they found relevant to this role and their background.

- Ask candidates to create a plan for their first quarter in the role using any format they wish.

- Give them this hypothetical: *If you had $10,000 to spend in your job over the next year, what would you spend it on?*

There are infinite ways to approach the problem and communicate the answer. You'll get a front-row seat to how they move through a nebulous challenge. It's their AQ in motion.

Managing for Agility

Can you guess the two most common reasons why people leave their jobs? The first, unsurprisingly, is having a bad manager. (This one, thankfully, is under your control.) The second reason employees leave is a lack of growth opportunities. This means that if you can support your team and provide chances for them to evolve, you'll have motivated employees who will persist through CHURN. In part 2, we discussed how the ABC's of Agility raise your AQ. They're also a helpful guide for how to show up for your team.

As you discovered in chapter 3, **anchors** ground us during times of turbulence. As a manager, your mission is to be your team's primary anchor. When there is a problem, they come to you. When things go sideways, they look to you. When they're confused or overwhelmed, you provide the clarity and calm to get back on track. The worst managers do the opposite—they make the situation worse by spinning their teams up into chaos. They escalate stress and make moments harder. How do you show up? Are you the stabilizer or the storm?

Once your team feels grounded and supported, you should also help them take **bets.**

This might look like scheduling big-idea brainstorms or dedicating team resources to taking bold swings. And when your team comes to you with ideas for change, don't default to no, even if it feels risky. Of course, as a manager, you can't greenlight every bet, but your job is to champion momentum, not suffocate it.

The **classroom** tool is the one that is the most essential to the manager mindset. Every interaction you have with your team, whether big or small, is the chance to teach. A one-on-one. A Slack thread. A project review. All of it is fertile ground for learning, and it's your job to ask incisive questions and recommend powerful resources. Most of all, create regular space for reflection for your employees. Commit to a biweekly or monthly cadence where the team pauses to ask: What are we learning? What is changing? How can we grow?

Finally, just as we saw with Phil Knight and Blue Ribbon Sports, great managers don't avoid discomfort—they reframe it. They remind their teams that any uncomfortable, destabilizing moment is a simple *wave* that will wash in and out, a *deviation from normal,* and a harbinger of positive change. Then in the lowest moments, when morale dips and stress spikes, they make it their mission to balance the stress with celebration, acknowledging the team's hard work with levity and recognition.

Managing as Your Archetype

Neurosurgeons are natural managers. They show up prepared, give thoughtful feedback, and possess a competent presence that swiftly earns trust. This diligence is a gift but also a risk. Left unchecked, it can turn into micromanagement. Trust goes both ways, and when your team sees that you believe in them, they'll rise to meet you.

Novelists, by contrast, often struggle with management. They're motivated by freedom and big ideas, preferring to lead through inspiration rather than supervision. They thrive on ideation and strategy, but they often avoid the daily grind of reviewing work or clarifying next steps. If you are a Novelist, your team needs more of you in the details. Not your brilliance alone, but also your presence. Take a cue from the Neurosurgeon and commit to showing up consistently, and not just when the work excites you.

Firefighters are beloved managers in crisis. They leap into the fray, extinguish chaos, and win the deep respect of their teams. But what happens when the fires die down? That's when the managerial effort wanes. Firefighters tend to disappear between emergencies, skipping check-ins and deprioritizing career development. To grow as managers, Firefighters must lead even amid calm and try their best to create it, too. This means establishing proactive check-ins and initiating discussions well before problems escalate.

Finally, Astronauts make unforgettable managers. Their passion is inspiring, and their authenticity is refreshing. They are encouraging leaders, pushing their teams to pivot, take risks, and dream. Their tendency, however, is to rush off toward adventure, while forgetting to take their team with them. The antidote is context, lots of context. Astronauts must loop their teams into their thought process and, above all, be patient, remembering that others may need time to catch up.

Small Deeds

What you've just read isn't a checklist or a rigid formula. It's a lens—a way to see your role as a manager through the eyes of agility. It's a nudge to notice how AQ can be found in every part of your day. If you're unsure of where to start, begin with yourself: Remember, you're not just a manager. You are also a blueprint, a yardstick, and a North Star. If you dedicate yourself to Full AQ, soon you'll find your team right alongside you.

CHAPTER 10

Green & Black Thinking

The test of a first-rate
intelligence is the
ability to hold two
opposed ideas in the mind
at the same time, and still
retain the ability to function.

—F. Scott Fitzgerald

In the previous chapter, we explored what it means to be a high-AQ manager. Now we turn to a powerful tool—essential for managers and employees seeking to thrive amid uncertainty. I call it *Green & Black Thinking*, a concept I developed from studying hundreds of founders and executives who consistently succeeded in the volatile conditions of CHURN.

To understand *Green & Black Thinking,* we must first look at the framework it draws from. In 1985, a cognitive theorist named Edward de Bono published a book called *The Six Thinking Hats* in which he introduced a simple yet transformative idea. He posited that we each have access to six distinct modes of thinking—six metaphorical "hats"—that shape how we perceive the world. Take, for instance, how I might describe where I live in New York City. My answer would vary depending on which hat I'm wearing.

The **white hat** is about *facts,* figures, and objective information. Through this lens, I'd describe my house factually as a "rental brownstone near Fort Greene Park in Brooklyn that was built in 1901." **Neurosurgeons** wear the white hat easily, because they take comfort in data, meticulously researching and gathering every relevant detail.

The opposite of the white hat is the **red hat,** which is about feelings and *emotions.* From this perspective, I'd describe my house as "a calm and cozy respite from the stress of city life." While this tells you nothing about the square footage or layout, it reveals something more personal: how the space makes me feel. Of all the Archetypes, **Astronauts** are the most aligned with the red hat, guided as they are by passion and emotional insight.

Then there's the **yellow hat,** sunny and *optimistic.* It highlights what's working—the benefits, upsides, and assets of the situation. Donning this hat, I'd list the best parts of my home, describing it as "the nicest place I've ever lived in New York City, with a chef's kitchen, stained glass windows, and plenty of room for our family." **Firefighters** and **Astronauts** both wear this hat well, buoyed by their natural glass-half-full outlook.

In contrast, the **black hat** is discerning and *critical.* It focuses on risks, limitations, and what might go wrong. Here, I would say, "The rent is outrageous, especially given the street noise, creaky floors, and plumbing issues." **Neurosurgeons** frequently reach for the black hat, as they are rigorous thinkers who scan for weak points and worst-case scenarios.

The **green hat,** like a sprouting plant, symbolizes growth and *creative possibility.* Through this lens, I'd dream about the future, stating, "I live in a brownstone in Brooklyn that I hope to buy and renovate in the next few years." Green is the hat of progress, and comes naturally for the **Firefighter,** who is an expert at creative problem-solving, and for the **Novelist,** who constantly imagines alternative futures. For them, putting on the green hat is intuitive.

Finally, the **blue hat** of *process* brings structure, organization, and strategy. With this mindset, I'd focus on the logistics and operations of my house, noting that "the lease runs from September to September, rent is due on the fifth, and trash is collected on Thursdays and Sundays." This organized way of thinking aligns with both the **Neurosurgeon's** and the **Novelist's** ways of thinking, as it relies on systems and plans.

Each Archetype favors one or two hats, but that doesn't mean that the others are out of reach. In fact, growing your AQ means learning to master all six hats, especially the ones that don't come as easily.

Figure 12: The Six Thinking Hats

Color	Style	A Description of Where I Live	Archetype
White	*Facts and figures*	A rental brownstone in Brooklyn, built in 1901	Neurosurgeon
Red	*Feelings*	A cozy, calm respite from the stress of the city	Astronaut
Yellow	*Optimism*	Stained glass, chef's kitchen, lots of space for our family	Astronaut and Firefighter
Black	*Criticism*	Creaky stairs, too much street noise, bad plumbing	Neurosurgeon
Green	*Creative possibility*	Maybe I could buy and renovate it one day	Firefighter and Novelist
Blue	*Process*	Rent due on the fifth; trash pickup on Thursdays and Sundays	Neurosurgeon and Novelist

Figure 12. Each hat represents a unique style of thinking that results in a singular way of perceiving the world. Notice how the description of my apartment in New York City changes dramatically, depending on which hat I wear.

I invite you to try on the hats yourself. Can you describe your own home, switching perspectives with each color? As a coach, I often ask my clients to do exactly that: cycle through the six hats to explore the varied dimensions of any given situation. This shifts them from their default way of seeing the world to fresh and surprising angles.

Not long ago, I facilitated an offsite session for a leadership team grappling with unresolved tension. They weren't collaborating well, and when CHURN arose, they'd clash even more. I used the *Six Thinking Hats* framework to get these feuding colleagues in alignment. We began with the **white hat,** naming only objective facts. Then came the **red hats,** as each person shared their fears, frustrations, and emotional truths. Once everyone felt heard, we moved to the **yellow** and **black hats** simultaneously, surfacing the team's strengths while candidly confronting its weaknesses.

Next came the **green hat** of creative ideation. The team brainstormed expansive new ways to work better together. Finally, we closed with the **blue hat** of process, organizing what was said, synthesizing insights, and aligning on next steps. In just the span of a morning, this formerly discordant team became unified and aligned.

If you make the effort, like that team did, to practice wearing all six of the hats, you'll raise your AQ in a flash. The most agile among us don't avoid the thinking hats that feel unnatural to them. Instead, they lean into them. I've seen dramatic growth in clients once they become comfortable switching hats with fluency.

One client, a former investor turned CEO, spent most of his professional life wearing the black and blue hats. He excelled at finding flaws, identifying risk (black), and building operational plans to address them (blue). When he launched his company, those strengths served him—costs dropped, margins improved, and the business ran with precision. But he didn't become an *exceptional* founder until he mastered the full set. By embracing the red, white, yellow, and green hats, he also learned to listen, motivate, build culture, and take big swings. That's agility in action.

If you want to grow your AQ, you must become skilled with all six of the hats, too. Relying on just one or two can leave you rigid and stuck. Let's pause and stock.

Which one or two hats do you wear most often in your daily work? Which ones do you avoid? Which two hats would be most valuable for you to practice? When you answer these questions and start adopting all six hats, you become nimble, responsive, and equipped for any situation.

Green & Black for Tough Times

While being able to alternate from one hat to another is important for high AQ, the combination of **Green & Black Thinking** is especially powerful in times of crisis. I'll explain how it works through the story of how NVIDIA nearly went out of business and what they did to save themselves.

NVIDIA was founded in 1993 by Jensen Huang, Chris Malachowsky, and Curtis Priem. While it's now a global leader in AI hardware and software, the company began with a different ambition: to build cutting-edge graphics chips for PC and console gaming. They launched at the peak of the gaming boom, an era defined by groundbreaking titles like *Doom* and *Wolfenstein 3D*, which rendered the flat, pixelated graphics of *Street Fighter* and *Mortal Kombat* instantly outdated. NVIDIA quickly secured funding from top-tier investors, and they weren't alone. Within a few months, eighty-nine other competitors had also raised capital to chase the same vision.

In 1995, NVIDIA looked like the frontrunner. They struck a

deal with Sega to provide the engines for their arcade games and their newest home console. They set the industry standards for 3D graphics chips, and they chose quadrilaterals, four-sided shapes, as their foundation. The best engineering talent in Silicon Valley flocked to NVIDIA, thrilled to work for the industry leader.

But by 1996, their early lead had vanished. What was once a first-mover advantage had become its greatest liability. Microsoft had entered the 3D graphics arena and adopted triangles—not quadrilaterals, as NVIDIA had, for its rendering standard. Overnight, NVIDIA's chips became incompatible with Microsoft application program interfaces (APIs), which the majority of game developers relied upon. Two major blows followed: NVIDIA's chips lacked sufficient memory compared to newer competitors, and Sega, their last lifeline, canceled their partnership. Within months, NVIDIA was left with a failing product, just $3 million in the bank, and only nine months of runway. Faced with a rapidly closing window, the co-founders weighed three options:

1. **Stay the course with their current chip.** The two co-founders in charge of technology, Chris and Curtis, preferred this option, since they already had one hundred loyal engineers who were invested in the current architecture. Any change from the existing strategy might put the whole tech team at risk.

2. **Give up on the plan and shut down or sell the company.** This is the practical route most entrepreneurs would've taken, since designing a new chip would take two years, and NVIDIA had just nine months of runway.

3. **Start over and design a brand-new chip.** Jensen,
   the CEO, wanted to pivot, but everyone else,
   including his co-founders, considered this path risky
   and likely impossible.

Before we reveal the path that NVIDIA chose, let's pair each of these options to one of the thinking hats. The first option, to stay the course, reflects classic *yellow hat thinking*: hopeful, optimistic, and focused on their strengths. In this case, NVIDIA could take comfort in its exceptional engineering team and distinctive technical vision.

The second option, to shut down or sell, embodies *black hat thinking*: cautious, realistic, and focused on minimizing loss. From this perspective, NVIDIA had already had one misstep, and with the odds stacked against them, any new strategy seemed as likely to fail.

The third option, the boldest move, represents both the *black* and *green hats*. It's a cold reckoning of past mistakes (black), followed by a creative leap into the future (green). This is the essence of *Green & Black Thinking,* and it's the path that NVIDIA ultimately chose.

Starting with the **black hat,** they faced reality. They acknowledged their strategic shortcomings, let go of 70 percent of their staff to extend their runway, and scrapped their failing chip. Then, with the **green hat,** Jensen proposed a radical solution: bypass the industry's two-year chip development cycle by testing the new design internally using a novel technology called an emulator. They spent a third of their remaining cash on this unproven tool, then designed a brand-new chip and ordered 100,000 units of it from the foundry without the standard back-and-forth testing. It was a massive gamble.

The result? The RIVA 128 chip arrived just months later. The final product, buggy and imperfect, supported only a fraction of the blend modes other chips did, but it was the best technology on the market. In the first four months, NVIDIA sold more than one million units. Within three years, NVIDIA went public. Two years after that, they surpassed $1 billion in annual revenue. Today, NVIDIA is worth more than $3 trillion and, at times, has been the most valuable company in the world. None of this would have been possible without Jensen's **Green & Black** mindset.

Reform School Beginnings

Green & Black Thinking isn't reserved for CEOs. Whether you're just starting your career, somewhere in the middle, or between roles entirely, this mindset is a powerful asset. In fact, Jensen Huang developed it long before becoming the CEO of NVIDIA. He was nine years old, to be precise. Let's step back in time.

When Jensen was growing up in Taiwan and Thailand, his father, determined to move the family to the United States one day, taught his children English from a dictionary—ten new words a day, every day. Unfortunately, the Huangs lacked the finances to move to America as a unit, but soon an unexpected opportunity emerged. It was Oneida Baptist Institute, a rare boarding school within the family's budget, and at the tender age of nine years old, Jensen moved to eastern Kentucky without his parents. He and his brother were the first foreigners to enroll in the school, and perhaps the first Asian people to ever live in the town. When they arrived, it quickly became clear why the tuition was so low. Oneida Baptist Institute was not a traditional boarding school but rather a reform school for troubled children. Jensen's roommate was a seventeen-year-old fresh from prison and covered in stab wounds from a knife fight.

I think of myself at age nine. I was in the fourth grade, and even though I was an independent kid, I can't imagine surviving in those circumstances. Jensen, however, thrived. He and his roommate, who was eight years his senior, became fast friends. Jensen helped him with math, and the roommate returned the favor by sharing his love of weight lifting. Although his two years at the school often involved cleaning latrines and getting beat up by other students, he remains grateful for his time there. "Now I don't get scared often," Huang said. "I don't worry about going places I haven't gone before, and I can tolerate a lot of discomfort." In 2019, with gratitude for his time at Oneida, Jensen and his wife, Lori, donated $2 million to the school.

Even at nine, Jensen practiced **Green & Black Thinking.** His green hat helped him imagine a new life in this strange, rough new environment. He saw possibility where others might only see isolation. He made friends, learned new skills, and found opportunity in discomfort. That's Full AQ in action. At the same time, he also wore the careful and diligent black hat. He followed the rules, steered clear of trouble, and navigated his new world with foresight. Decades later, when NVIDIA faced near-certain failure, Jensen didn't flinch. The mindset that helped him to thrive in tumult as a child did the same for him as an adult. Green & Black Thinking is about holding two strong points of view that seemingly contradict each other. It's **dreaming boldly** (*green hat*) while also **preparing for the worst** (*black hat*). It's **reaching high** (*green hat*) while **keeping your feet firmly planted** (*black hat*).

When you learn to think this way, like Jensen did, you unlock a rare and powerful combination: possibility and pragmatism. You're visionary *and* detail-oriented, self-confident *and* self-critical, and that is exactly the right mindset to solve huge issues with agility.

The Fountain of Youth

What would it take for you to stay in your current career until the age of 108? For me, this would mean sixty-nine more years of coaching, writing, giving talks, and running a business. I'd be working while my now-infant daughter grows up and starts her own career and family, and I'd probably still be going when her kids have their first children, too. I'd be a centenarian checking emails, typing away between coaching calls, still immersed in the work I began decades earlier. It's hard to imagine not getting exhausted, burned out, or bored at some point.

Yet Irving Kahn did exactly that. He was the world's oldest active investor, starting his career at age 23 and working until he was 108. Over the course of eighty-five years, he managed a financial portfolio that grew to $1 billion through the Great Depression, the 1970s oil crisis, the dot-com crash of 2000, and the Great Recession. He loved his work up until the very end, taking a taxi to his office each morning to meet with his team. Irving Kahn pulled off the impossible—he had a long-lasting yet ever-changing career. He did it with *Green & Black Thinking*.

His **green hat** kept him curious, optimistic, and future-focused. In his late fifties, he advocated for greater accountability and credentialing for investors, and he was among the first class of applicants to sit for the now-standard certified financial analyst (CFA) exam. Today, hundreds of thousands of people take it every year. When he was seventy-three, he founded his own investment fund, the Kahn Brothers Group, and well into his eighties and nineties, he read three newspapers a day, broadened to a Kindle e-reader, and kept expanding his knowledge. In 2008, at 103 years old, he guided his firm through the Great Recession—a fitting bookend for a career that began in the Great Depression.

Irving was also as **black hat** as they come. He scrutinized every piece of company reporting, dissected economic data, and dismissed his looser peers who jumped into the market based on hype, without enough thoughtfulness. Irving trusted his instinct (*green hat*), but only when backed by rigorous research (*black hat*). That balance of belief and skepticism allowed him to invest counter to the crowd and win.

Looking back, it's clear: Green & Black Thinking gave Irving both passion and endurance. The *green hat* fueled excitement, while the *black hat* sustained discipline. Green & Black Thinking can be a fountain of youth for all of us, keeping us optimistic enough to leap and grounded enough to do so safely. This is especially critical when it comes to new technology that intersects with our work, whether AI, Web3, or no-code platforms. Wearing the green hat, we hold unfettered possibility as we experiment broadly with what the technology can do, but we also wear the black hat to stay alert to bugs, blind spots, and ethical questions. We use Green & Black Thinking to become early yet perceptive adopters.

Now let's turn your attention back to your own career, as you consider these questions:

- What surprising or unconventional decisions have you made with the **green hat** on?

- What thoughtful, well-researched decisions have come from your **black hat**?

- Bring to mind the single largest issue, challenge, or uncertainty in your work right now. What would the **green hat** do? How about the **black hat**? How can you pursue both strategies simultaneously?

Green & Black Thinking doesn't become instinctual overnight. For most of us, it will take intentional practice. Remember, **Firefighters** and **Novelists** are already naturals at green hat thinking—you see possibility in chaos and are drawn to reinvention. So, if you're one of these two Archetypes, your job is to invest in your black hat: to pause, assess risk, and think through consequences. Try building in premortem conversations (what *might* go wrong) and postmortem discussions (what *did* go wrong). Your mission is to befriend skepticism, risk mitigation, and critique.

If you're a **Neurosurgeon,** the opposite is true. You're already adept at planning precision—which is black hat territory. Your challenge is to dream more freely. Begin each project by imagining the best-case scenario. Schedule brainstorming sessions about the big swings you could take, and surround yourself with case studies that stretch your sense of what's possible.

If you're an **Astronaut,** you're already fluent in the yellow hat of positivity. Your next challenge is to strengthen both the green and black hats. To get better at the black hat, borrow from the strategies outlined for the Firefighter and the Novelist: Carve out time for thoughtful, detail-oriented work that grounds you in realism. To grow your green hat of creative problem-solving, you'll need to loosen your attachment to your original vision.

Sometimes, your path isn't the only or best way forward. Creativity thrives not just in vision, but in collaboration and adaption.

Yes, there is work to do, no matter your Archetype. The good news is that with Full AQ, you can move fluidly among all six hats, slipping them on and off as needed. Then, in the most difficult moments, you can wear two at once, green and black, to remain hopeful and prepared, inventive and grounded. That's what agility looks like.

CHAPTER 11

Bushwhack Like a Camel

Life shrinks or expands in
proportion to one's courage.

—Anaïs Nin

Camels walked a long way to get to where they are today. While most of the world's dromedaries now roam across Africa and the Middle East, their journey began with a group of intrepid ancestors who had the courage to leave North America and cross the Bering Land Bridge seventeen thousand years ago. Yes, the world's very first camels hailed from that snowy place that we now know as Canada.

How could this be? I wondered, having always thought of camels as custom-made for the scorching desert, where we find them today. After all, the fat in their humps gets converted to water, their triple eyelids protect them from dust storms, and the shape of their toes makes for graceful sand trekking. It turns out these features were originally adaptations for the cold North American climate. Their fat humps work excellently for the winter, too, and those triple eyelids and lively toes are great for blizzards and the snow.

These days, camels are no longer native to North America. You won't find them grazing with musk oxen or traversing the Rocky Mountain foothills. This is because the last of the Canadian camels died out twelve thousand years ago during the Quaternary megafauna extinction, alongside other mammals like the mastodon and the European lion. We'd never know the splendor of camels if it weren't for that brave caravan who carved out a new path. If they'd remained only in North America, they'd now be relegated to the wisps of history.

As the world's climate changes exponentially, many modern-day species face their own camel-like crossroads, deciding whether to abandon their traditional, precarious homes for uncertain fates in new places. Take penguins, for instance. Some species, like the Adélie and Chinstrap penguins, have decided to stay put with rigid dedication to their historical nesting spots. Despite the changes to their ecosystem, they are firmly entrenched in the Avoidant Stage of AQ, clinging to the status quo. Others, like the Gentoo penguin, are more agile, happy to jettison their old nests as they move southward, embracing their shifting world with Full AQ. Unsurprisingly, the rigid penguins, stuck in the past, are declining rapidly, while the penguins with AQ are flourishing, growing in many multiples every year. From camels and penguins, whose job it is to evolve and survive, there's a lesson here for all of us in our professional lives.

In times of great change, upheaval, and uncertainty, we must think like a camel and learn the skill of Bushwhacking, which means carving a path where none exists. Bushwhacking is what it looks like to reach the Full AQ Stage, and it is a hallmark of those who succeed in uncertain times.

Laundry Washer to Bank President

Bushwhacking is the ability to create a route where none existed before. If you've ever walked through a dense, untamed forest, you know how physically demanding it is—and if you've ever been the first to do anything (first in your family to go to college, first of your friends to work in engineering, first woman executive at your company), you know how mentally, emotionally, and symbolically difficult Bushwhacking can be, too. It's infinitely more work to forge a path through inhospitable, unwelcoming terrain than to stroll down a well-worn, clear-cut route. The former requires strength, resilience, and imagination, while the latter merely asks for your time and energy. It's the difference between trekking a thousand kilometers across the Bering Land Bridge with Full AQ versus grazing a familiar pasture like a typical camel. Neither option is easy per se, but Bushwhacking requires far greater fortitude, and few people embody this more than Maggie Lena Walker.

If you ever feel that life has stacked the deck against you, consider the odds Maggie Lena Walker faced. She was the daughter of a formerly enslaved woman named Elizabeth Draper and a white father, and she arrived in this world just after the Civil War ended. Back then, in Richmond, Virginia, where Maggie was raised, it was a crime for people of different races to be romantically or sexually intimate, and it would remain illegal for another century after her birth. As you can imagine, her early circumstances left her very few choices. At the age of eleven, she began working as a laundress alongside her mother to help support the family. "I was not born with a silver spoon in my mouth," she said, "but with a laundry basket practically upon my head."

Had Maggie not learned to Bushwhack, her life might have followed one of just a few narrow paths. Free Black women in Virginia in the late 1800s could be factory workers, street vendors, or domestic laborers, like maids, cooks, or nannies. In the best-case scenario, and with a lot of hard work and luck, Maggie might have become a teacher, but by law, she'd have to leave the profession if she ever married. In her lifetime, Maggie did indeed work as a domestic laborer and as a teacher, but in 1902, at the age of thirty-nine, she did something unprecedented: She became the first female bank president in American history. How did she do it? To answer this question, we must understand what it means to Bushwhack through the lens of Maggie's extraordinary career.

Dreaming

Let's return to our animal examples for a moment, because Bushwhacking begins with dreaming. If the Bering Land Bridge camels and Gentoo penguins exemplify Bushwhacking, then Keiko the orca, introduced in part 2, stands as their foil. If you recall, after decades in captivity, Keiko took part in a rehabilitation program designed to reintroduce him to the wild. In many ways, the effort succeeded. He learned to catch his own fish, swim thousands of miles alone, and call out to other orcas. Unfortunately, what he gained in his skills, he lacked in his dreams. A lifetime in captivity had dulled his imagination. Even with the freedom and ability to go anywhere, Keiko chose a busy tourist port, seeking human affection, and he re-created the unnatural conditions of his amusement park life.

I think we can all relate to Keiko when it comes to our professions. We can be extremely competent, talented, and even agile in acquiring skills, but if our imaginations are limited, we may never believe that more is possible. Even when we're capable of Bushwhacking, we hesitate to try. That's why Bushwhacking begins with dreaming. Desire must come before effort. To break down a door, you must first wonder what lies behind it, and then find the strength to accomplish the feat.

Maggie Lena Walker's ability to dream came from a defiant inner voice that asked, "Why not me?" At sixteen, while still in school, she joined the Independent Order of St. Luke, a fraternal society that provided its members with insurance to pay for the burial costs of their loved ones. She rose through the ranks by initiating bold new ideas—establishing a youth division, launching a newspaper, opening an emporium, and founding a bank. Many of her ideas were inspired by other fraternal societies that were thriving at the time. She saw what they had achieved, and even if they faced fewer race and gender barriers than she did, she still wondered, "Why not me?" After all, she thought, her community was just as deserving and capable.

To spark the dreaming mode of Bushwhacking in your own life, follow Maggie's lead and ask yourself the simple question "Why not me?" If other people have accomplished the future you want, why shouldn't you? This mindset is especially important in the early stages of your career, when you may hear from naysayers, well-intentioned or not, warning you off your big dreams. I remember those voices. Early in my career in recruiting, I was cautioned against trying to pivot into broader operations. Later, when I dreamed of becoming a leadership coach, a respected coach warned me, "It will be an uphill battle with your background." I know he meant well. He was simply wearing the black hat of pragmatism. But had I listened, I would have missed out on this career I've excelled in.

You may hear similarly disheartening feedback as you explore your own career ambitions. You may even hear it from the people closest to you. (On my thirty-fifth birthday, I told a few friends that I wanted to write two books by the time I was forty, and my friends—all ambitious and kind people—were vocally skeptical. It turns out they were wrong, because I just did it.) Remember, even if others' imaginations are limited, yours need not be, too.

This mindset of dreaming isn't just for sweeping career shifts or writing books—it applies to daily tasks and responsibilities, too. Whether you're launching a project, improving a system, or offering a new idea, let your imagination lead you. When your colleagues insist it won't work, don't be deterred. Roll up your sleeves and find out for yourself.

On the flip side, if you're further along in your career, and a younger person shares a dream with you, don't squash it. Offer reality, yes—but not discouragement. Don't be the reason someone decides not to try.

Dreaming is the beginning of Bushwhacking, and for many it takes practice. If you've spent years in the Fighting Stage, internalizing negativity, your dreams may feel unrealistic or out of reach. That's okay. Start by shifting to Full AQ thinking and focus on seeing the world through its expansive, positive, and unemotional lens.

It helps, too, to surround yourself with dreamers. Your Astronaut and Novelist friends are naturally wired to imagine futures that others can't yet see. Their brave perspective may be the perfect antidote for when, like Keiko, you're held back by old beliefs. As you flex your dreaming muscles, let Maggie Lena Walker be your North Star. If a Black woman born in post–Civil War Virginia could strive for a future no one else could see, then you can, too. Try it now by reflecting on these prompts:

1. What is a dream career you want but don't yet believe is possible?

2. What is something hard you've already accomplished, despite others doubting you?

3. Open your Agility Journal and write down your dream career path in vivid detail. When you finish, write the words "Why not me?" at the top of the page.

Bushwhacking Bets

Once you've cleared the hurdle of dreaming, you can begin taking action and moving forward. Let's explore what Bushwhacking, the act of forging your own path, looks like. In 1899, when Maggie Lena Walker took over the Independent Order of St. Luke, it was on the brink of collapse. It had a dwindling population of about one thousand members, sizable debt, and just $31.61 in its treasury. If any of us took over such a poorly resourced organization, we might be afraid to take risks and try to conserve assets instead. But Maggie was braver than most; rather than play it safe, she made bets. She tried out new strategies, made decisions with incomplete information, and took risks. She went where no independent order had gone before.

First, Maggie led a massive recruiting drive with a focus on African American women. It was rare for independent orders to even admit women as members, so this recruitment strategy was especially novel. Next, she overhauled the order's insurance policies to make them both more economically sustainable and more appealing to members. She'd never worked in the insurance industry, but Maggie didn't let this stop her from figuring it out as she went along. Finally, she built personal relationships, not just with other Black business leaders but with white allies, too. Both groups helped her achieve the extraordinary feat of securing a bank charter for the St. Luke Penny Savings Bank. Under Maggie's leadership, the order's membership grew to seventy thousand, an extraordinary eightyfold increase, and they expanded their insurance fund to $8 million, a remarkable feat for an under-resourced organization that had struggled for years.

As you can see from Maggie's story, the essence of Bushwhacking is taking bets. Remember, a bet is any time you take action despite not knowing the outcome. If you're at the beginning (or a new beginning) of your professional journey, make a bet to expand your professional network by joining affiliation groups or inviting a stranger to coffee. Invest in Durable Skills, like influence and persuasion, or take a good hard look at how you can improve your self-confidence. If you're already established in your career, bet by taking a chance on an unexpected hire for your team, or by trying out a brand-new technology. Any of these acts count as Bushwhacking when you're forging a path that you haven't walked before. If you're wondering what Stage of AQ describes your career, ask yourself if you've Bushwhacked lately. If it's been some time since you charted an unfamiliar course, then chances are you're stuck in either the Avoidant Stage or the Fighting Stage.

If you're wondering how to get out of a rut and back to Full AQ, ask yourself these three questions:

1. How am I currently staying on a conventional, well-trodden path? (the Avoidant Stage)

2. What are three ways I could veer off that path? (the Fighting Stage)

3. What is one step I can take now to improve my positivity and optimism? (the Full AQ Stage)

Fixing

Bushwhacking isn't just setting a new path—it requires mainte-nance, which we call *fixing*. Over Maggie Lena Walker's thirty-five-year tenure as the head of the Independent Order of St. Luke, she had to constantly fix and reroute the paths she'd laid. For instance, in 1905, the order opened an emporium that sold household items like clothing and furniture to the Black commu-nity in Richmond. This business perfectly complemented Mag-gie's vision of economic self-sufficiency for African Americans. Unfortunately, the white emporium owners in the area did not take well to the competition, and after years of pressure, Maggie made the tough decision to close the store in 1911, recognizing that the path she'd forged six years before needed amending.

The same was true for the order's bank. The St. Luke Penny Savings Bank thrived for decades, but in the 1930s, amid the Great Depression, Maggie saw that a change was needed, and she set off to merge her organization with two other Black-owned banks. While this strategy was never in her original design, Maggie understood that fixing the path is an important element of Bushwhacking.

To get really good at fixing, we have to stop tolerating what's broken, whether big or small. This came up during a casual conversation with one of my clients, when we both realized that we had simultaneously lived in the same apartment building before we knew each other. We discussed the doorman we both loved, Humberto, the eyesore stack of packages that always sat in the lobby, and the fire that had consumed the seventh floor in one of the years we overlapped. I asked him if he'd liked his apartment, and he told me a story about when he first moved in. It had a beautiful view, he said. From the eighteenth floor, he could see clear across Manhattan, but there was a downside. His apartment sat above the roof of one of NYU's dorms, which was covered with long rows of air-conditioner condensers. One of them was broken and made a pinging noise that my client could hear from his apartment every time the fan circled around.

That building was a tall one, with twenty-one floors, and a whole line of other apartments was also in earshot of the persistent pinging. My client contacted the superintendent of our building. "Oh yes," the super said. "We've had a lot of complaints about this over the years, but there's nothing we can do because NYU owns the building. You'll get used to it, and you won't even notice it soon," he assured him. My client, however, did not listen. He found the email address of the NYU facilities team and shot off a quick note about the issue. Twenty minutes later, my client watched from his window as a member of NYU's maintenance staff came onto the roof, fiddled with the condenser for a couple of minutes, and silenced a yearslong annoyance.

After he finished the story, I smiled at my client. "That's why you're great at your job," I said. And it was true. This small moment was indicative of a general personality trait that all of us must work to cultivate—a bias to action when it comes to fixing problems. Think about how many issues, big and small, we encounter at work but willingly ignore: the recurring meeting with no point, the outdated informational materials, the buggy database. They work well enough, we think, and we tolerate these nuisances and push down our annoyance until it seems like every system, process, or relationship at the office is a little bit broken.

When a once-clear trail devolves into a weedy, overgrown route, we must be willing to spring into action and fix the issue, no matter how many times we've revised it in the past. With the expert Bushwhacker's spirit, we remind ourselves that *the fun is in the fixing*. Forging a new trail is deeply satisfying work, but so, too, is maintaining it.

Bushwhacking Yesterday and Today

Today's world is very different from the century that Maggie Lena Walker inhabited. There is more legal and social support for gender equality, and there are more possibilities for people of color. However, many of the career paths from the last few decades have been wiped off the map. A college degree no longer guarantees a good job, and even higher education, like a JD or an MBA, is not a straight line to success. Modern life is far too unstable, unpredictable, and laden with change to trust that pre-made paths will endure. That's why we must all be Bushwhackers. The trails behind us are disappearing, and it is our job to create new ones.

Building a career in the future doesn't just mean more uncertainty—it also means greater sameness. As AI takes over more and more of our thinking responsibilities, like writing our memos and planning our strategy, many of our outputs will begin to look eerily similar. The originality of our thinking will decline. Our quirky ideas, lateral leaps, and non sequitur solutions will become rarer. The danger is clear: We risk peddling the same solid but uninspired, AI-generated thinking. The antidote to the sameness of AI is Bushwhacking, which forces you to think for yourself and forge a bespoke path. If you want to stand out from the crowd in a homogeneous world, let Bushwhacking be your superpower.

Now let's raise our AQ by Bushwhacking together. Answer the questions below and write them in your Agility Journal:

1. What is a *dream* that you want to turn into a possibility?

2. What is one action you can take to start *Bushwhacking* a new trail?

3. What's one quick *fix* you can make? For example, does a system, process, or pattern at work need revision?

Summary of Part 3:
The Great Equalizer

My desire to reinvent myself began in earnest when I was ten. My family didn't have money—that much was obvious. We lived in Section 8 housing, I was skinny as a rail, and I appeared so neglected that an elementary school teacher opened up an investigation. There was nothing I could do to change these facts, but it occurred to me that if people believed that I was smart, perhaps they'd overlook that I was poor. Finally, here was something in my chaotic childhood that I might actually be able to control.

This was when I first became particular about my grammar. I was a stickler for how to answer the simple question "How are you?" If I heard anyone, adult or child, stranger or relative, respond with the words "I'm doing good," I'd shout, "It's an adverb! You're not doing *good*. You're doing *well*." I harped on the difference between *less* and *fewer* and was smug about the right use of the subjunctive. My goal was to appear proper, educated, and exact, even if my home life was mayhem.

My desire to be perceived as intelligent only became stronger as I grew older. I read Dostoyevsky and Nabokov, I memorized poetry, and I skimmed issues of *The Atlantic* at the library. I read voraciously, not to follow my interests, but to craft an identity as a "smart person." Most of my decisions and actions, both big and small, came from my drive to signal IQ. *Fake it till you make it,* I thought, *and leave your childhood far behind you.*

It mostly worked. I grew into a polished and knowledgeable adult who interviewed well. I was a structured thinker and a crisp communicator, and I could synthesize complex information on the fly. I led with my IQ, and this eventually earned me a seat at a top venture capital firm alongside Ivy League MBAs. But it wasn't IQ that helped me keep that seat. It was my AQ.

"I'll do it" was my response whenever my boss needed a volunteer.

"Let me take a stab at it," I'd say, when it came to new projects.

"Yes, of course I know how," I'd announce with confidence, only to spend all night teaching myself the ropes.

I switched strategies from IQ to AQ because I knew that I could no longer compete on pure IQ alone. My colleagues had been raised from birth to understand business models and advanced logic. They had the best training, top schooling, and coveted internships—none of which I had—so I put myself on a different, nimbler track. I took big bets, I learned constantly, I jumped into discomfort, and in the process I gained my advantage where it mattered most—my AQ.

Don't get me wrong: IQ matters, and so does EQ, but as our world further tips into constant instability, AQ becomes the primary accelerant. IQ might get you in the door, as it did for me, but AQ is what decides whether or not you'll succeed. According to a study in the *Journal of Managerial Issues,* employees with high learning agility were promoted more and got higher salary increases than their peers with low learning agility. Similarly, a study by Christopher Lee Bedford from the University of Minnesota confirmed that agility is not only a distinct entity apart from intelligence but also a better predictor of an employee's potential for career advancement.

These days, I am more relaxed about grammar, and I've stopped trying to look smart. I no longer care about signaling intelligence, no matter how much I want to impress someone. Now the one thing I want everyone to know about me is that I'm agile. I lead with my AQ. So, I ask questions, I take risks, and I try new things. I am open-minded, curious, and game for whatever comes next.

The beautiful thing about AQ is that it's free. You don't need an advanced degree or costly training to signal your high AQ to others. All you have to do is live it. Unlike IQ, AQ can't be faked. Either you practice agility or you don't. And that's why it's the great equalizer. You can come from anywhere and become a high-AQ person, and this will pave the way for your success.

These days, Full AQ is the new college degree. So, cultivate AQ and seek it out in others. Don't waste your time analyzing someone's grammar or what's on their résumé. Instead, pay attention to what really matters—namely, **Durable Skills, Green & Black Thinking,** and the ability to **Bushwhack.** These are the professional skills for our unstable world, and you must master them as if your life depends on it—because, as a matter of fact, it does. My hope is that you'll start to use this new suite of skills and mindsets. Practice them at home, too. The reality of this world is that home and work life now blur together, but luckily, as Jensen Huang's reform school experience shows, the agility we breed in our private lives shows up at the office, too.

The Full AQ Life

To improve is to change;
so to be perfect is to have changed often.

—Winston Churchill

Whenever I struggle to maintain Full AQ, I realize how lucky I am. I'm lucky because there's an agility expert living in my house, and she shows me how to raise my AQ any time I look at her. As you'll remember, Shunryu Suzuki said, "Everything changes," and my infant daughter, Taia, with her two-toothed grin, is living proof. In just one year, her brain has doubled in size. She's gone from supine and inert to zooming around. Her liquid diet has been replaced by hands shoveling food, and now she can sleep, really sleep, soothing herself back to slumber after needing me so much before.

One day, I was shocked to hear her first word after the requisite *Dada*. "Turta!" she said, as she grabbed her palm-sized turtle stuffie. Then it was "Turta!" again when she spotted a cartoon turtle on the carpet of the local library. One week later, she saw a real-life version at the Brooklyn Children's Museum, and again, she knew. "Turta!" she said, and I laughed as I watched her language ability bloom like spring flowers.

Of course, Taia is not unique. All children are born agile, and they hone their AQ as they develop. By age five, a child's brain is 90 percent fully grown, and by age ten they've learned twenty thousand words, with twenty more discovered every single day. As the nineteenth-century philosopher and psychologist William James wisely observed, "In youth we may have an absolutely new experience, subjective or objective, every hour of the day." For children, change and newness aren't disruptions; rather, they are the easy rhythm of life. They were born with the capacity to thrive amid CHURN, and this innate agility is good news for all of us, no matter our age. We were born with AQ. We've always needed it to survive. It's much more than a personality trait: Agility is our birthright.

The Agile Life

Because my professional interests sit squarely in the corporate world, I envisioned this book as a workplace guide. I hoped that managers would use the language within it to coach their teams, and employees and organizations alike would be happier and more effective for it. This is why part 3, the final section of this book, is laser-focused on the domain of our work. However, it was only as I simultaneously wrote and applied the concepts to my own life that I learned how far AQ can reach. I wrote this book for ambitious people who want to thrive in their careers, but, I suppose, I also wrote it for myself.

In the calendar year I spent writing this book, I brought Taia into the world, moved homes, launched a business, changed book publishers, got pregnant again, had a miscarriage, faced family conflict, lost a friend to suicide, and restarted therapy. That's several moments of big CHURN in one twelve-month period, and there were many nights when I cried, and one when I could not get off the floor, but I continued writing and this book served as a life raft. I trusted that AQ would carry me to solid ground, and thankfully it did. I invite you to lean on this book with the same depth of trust whenever you encounter CHURN in your life. The wind may remain uncontrollable and tumultuous, but now you have the ability to adjust your sails. You have the knowledge you need. Now let's put it all together.

We began this book with a list of predicaments we find ourselves in that AQ can fix. Let's pair each one with a unique solution that you've just learned by reading this book.

Predicament	Agility Antidote
You've been bombarded by change and burned out by change fatigue.	You tune in to your **Archetype** to understand what precisely is creating this discomfort for you. You seek out loved ones of different Archetypes who can help you.
You want to make a big shift but don't know how to begin.	You begin with the **ABC's.** You create **anchors,** you take **bets,** you adopt a mindset of **classroom,** and you accept **discomfort.** These skills jump-start you into action.
Your profession is changing around you, and you wonder what you should do.	Like Jensen Huang or Irving Kahn, you use your **Green & Black Thinking** to plan your next move with equal parts diligence and optimism.
It's been a while since you've learned a new skill.	You prioritize cultivating your **Durable Skills.** You know the investment is worth it because they will endure no matter how your life changes.
You feel left behind by changes in the people around you.	You consider whether you and the people around you might be on different **Stages of AQ,** then take steps to bridge the gap.
You experience anger, grief, or disappointment when the unexpected strikes.	You remind yourself about the **Full AQ Stage** and do whatever it takes to get back in that **logical, unemotional, and thankful** mindset.
You're unsure of what the future holds for you.	You get comfortable with moving through unknown terrain by practicing **Bushwhacking.** You create a new path for yourself.

Nonlinear Growth

It looks tidy in a chart, but real life is rarely linear. Growth is inherently messy. There will be breakthroughs, then regressions. Some days, you'll feel like you're soaring in the Full AQ Stage. Then an emergency crashes in and throws you right back to the Avoidant Stage. That's okay. The true marker of agility is not how you first react, but how you recover and bring yourself back to Full AQ.

Your relationship with this book won't be exactly linear either. Yes, you've arrived now at the conclusion, but your journey isn't ending. Keep this book on your desk, by your bedside, or even in your car. Designed as a reference, it's not just for reading cover to cover. That's why it includes charts and exercises for a hit of AQ on the go. When a moment of big CHURN shakes you up, consult part 2 and the ABC's. When life feels overwhelming, turn to the Stages, and if you find yourself in conflict with someone, the Archetypes can help you have a more thoughtful conversation.

It's easier to increase your AQ when you work with others. On this book's website, we offer discussion guides for book clubs and accountability groups, which you can use both at home and in the office. Even if you're not one for social engagements, you'll still benefit from sharing your process with others—your best friend, your partner, or even a parent. When you boost your AQ, you see the world through a new lens, and it helps to have someone looking with you.

I'll leave you with a final agility tip: ***Put it into words***. When you verbally acknowledge the agility in yourself and others, you'll find yourself surrounded by Full AQ people, because what we speak is what we create. Compliment your colleagues on their agility when you see it. Note your teammate's agility on a performance review, and when you see growth in yourself, boast a bit.

When your AQ is low, words can lift you back up to your innate agility. All you need to do is recall the mottoes below:

EVERYTHING CHANGES, AND I EMBRACE IT.
I LOVE CHANGE, AND CHANGE LOVES ME.
THE FUTURE IS COMING, AND I AM READY FOR IT.

Welcome to the world of Full AQ.

Acknowledgments

Thank you to my agent, Lynn Johnston, for offering the black hat thinking that sharpens my green hat. Lynn, I've been lucky to have you at my side as I bushwhacked my way through this book—and the last one, too.

I'm equally grateful to Amy Li, my visionary and generative editor. Amy, to call you an *editor* doesn't begin to capture your role. You are insightful, creative, and the most formidable of thought partners. You told me early on, "I meet my authors halfway," and you honored that through every revision.

I'm also thankful for the rest of the Penguin Random House team, including Paul Whitlach, Tara Gilbride, and Keely Brewer. A special thank-you to my speaking agent, Kate Berner, who helped bring AQ to thousands of people before it existed on the page. Kate, thank you for your thoughtful collaboration and for amplifying my voice.

There are many other people, far more talented than I, who lent their genius to this work. Anna and Rodrigo Corral, thank you for this exceptional cover. You approached the process not as a project, but as art, and it elevated my own relationship to this book. I owe a great debt to Maureen Clark, who copyedited this manuscript. Maureen, the time I spent with your notes was a master class in writing, and the effects will carry forward to every line I craft in the future. Thank you, also, to Barbara Cave Henricks and Melissa Connors for their strategy and care in launching this book into the world.

They say writing is a solitary pursuit, but I never felt that, thanks to my people anchors—especially Nikki D'Ambrosio, an Astronaut archetype through and through. Nikki, thank you for being the glue that holds the disparate pieces of my work together.

To my compatriots in writing, Piera Gelardi, Lydia Pang, and Carla Fernandez—our thousands of messages and voice notes gave me the dopamine hits that carried me through to the end. Thank you for dreaming and believing alongside me. Thank you to my friends—Sophia Li, Liya Shuster-Bier, Dolores O'Connor, Julia Pontecorvo, Lauren Shirley, Amir Sharif, Victoria Rogers, Owen Laub, Anouk Dey, and Cam Tudhope—for lending your robust minds to our AQ conversations.

The true origin of my AQ journey dates back generations, to my grandparents, Lê Thị Lý and Phạm Văn Đồng, who not only taught me agility but also instilled in me a love for reading and writing. This book wouldn't exist without their early influence— or the continued inspiration of my brother, Andrew Tran, my persistent role model for creative life.

Finally, to my husband, the brilliant Dev Aujla—thank you for reading everything I wrote (more than once), for sharing your enviable ease with words, and for spending this decade showing me what high AQ looks like. You are the Firefighter archetype, and I'm grateful to you for always being there to save the day. I may have dedicated this book to Taia, but I wrote it for you, for us, and for our family. To practice agility in life is a gift—and to do it with you is my greatest joy.

Notes

INTRODUCTION • AQ: Two Letters, Substantial Meaning

1   **"The beginning of wisdom":** Quoted in Barbara
    Tannenbaum, "The Importance of Names," California
    Academy of Sciences, January 22, 2013, https://www
    .calacademy.org/explore-science/the-importance-of-names.

2   **Daniel Gilbert, a professor:** Jordi Quoidbach, Daniel T.
    Gilbert, and Timothy D. Wilson, "The End of History
    Illusion," *Science* 339, no. 6115 (January 4, 2013): 96–98,
    https://dtg.sites.fas.harvard.edu/Quoidbach%20et%20al
    %202013.pdf.

2   **We change as much:** Mathew A. Harris et al., "Personality
    Stability from Age 14 to Age 77 Years," *Psychology and Aging*
    31, no. 8 (December 2016): 862–74, https://pmc.ncbi.nlm
    .nih.gov/articles/PMC5144810/.

3 **because of the *status quo bias*:** William Samuelson and Richard Zeckhauser, "Status Quo Bias in Decision Making," *Journal of Risk and Uncertainty* 1, no. 1 (March 1988): 7–59, https://doi.org/10.1007/bf00055564.

4 **The members of Gen Z:** "Job Mobility Is on the Minds of Young Workers," McCrindle, accessed August 20, 2025, https://mccrindle.com.au/article/job-mobility-is-on-the -minds-of-young-workers/.

4 **Formerly secure positions:** Kweilin Ellingrud et al., "Generative AI and the Future of Work in America," McKinsey & Company, July 26, 2023, https://www.mckinsey .com/mgi/our-research/generative-ai-and-the-future-of -work-in-america.

4 **In 1958, the average lifespan:** John C. Kelleher and Tim Koller, "How CFOs Can Adopt a VC Mindset: Staircase Ventures' Janet Bannister," *McKinsey on Finance* 84 (December 2023): 13, https://www.mckinsey.com/capabilities/strategy -and-corporate-finance/our-insights/how-cfos-can-adopt-a -vc-mindset-staircase-ventures-janet-bannister.

6 **in the late 1800s:** Elisabetta Cicciola, "Alfred Binet e le prime 'misure' dell'intelligenza (1905–1908)" [Alfred Binet and the First "Measures" of Intelligence (1905–1908)], *Physis: Rivista Internazionale di Storia della Scienza* 45, no. 1–2 (2008): 165–203.

6 **Lewis Terman, who transformed:** H. L. Minton, *Lewis M. Terman: Pioneer in Psychological Testing* (New York University Press, 1988).

6 **Terman believed that high IQ:** Katherine Duggan and Howard Friedman, "Genetic Studies of Genius and the Life Cycle Follow-Ups," in *The Encyclopedia of Adulthood and Aging*, ed. Susan Krauss Whitbourne (Wiley, 2015), 2:564–67, https://doi.org/10.1002/9781118521373.wbeaa200.

7   **The vast majority:** Richard C. Paddock, "The Secret IQ
Diaries: They Were Guinea Pigs in the Longest-Running
Psychological Study Ever, Their Identities Largely Kept a
Mystery. Now in Their 80s, the 'Children' of Lewis Terman
Are Still Defining What It Really Means to Be a Genius," *Los
Angeles Times,* July 30, 1995, https://www.latimes.com
/archives/la-xpm-1995-07-30-tm-29325-story.html.

7   **two future Nobel laureates:** Russell T. Warne et al., "Low
Base Rates and a High IQ Selection Threshold Prevented
Terman from Identifying Future Nobelists," *Intelligence* 82
(September 2020): 101488, https://doi.org/10
.1016/j.intell.2020.101488.

7   **Peter Salovey and John Mayer:** Peter Salovey and John D.
Mayer, "Emotional Intelligence," *Imagination, Cognition and
Personality* 9, no. 3 (March 1990): 185–211, https://doi.org
/10.2190/dugg-p24e-52wk-6cdg.

7   **Daniel Goleman popularized it:** Dana Ackley, "Emotional
Intelligence: A Practical Review of Models, Measures, and
Applications," *Consulting Psychology Journal: Practice and Research*
68, no. 4 (December 2016): 269–86, https://doi.org/10.1037
/cpb0000070.

7   **Corporations invested in EQ:** Rebecca Dickason et al., "A
History of Emotional Intelligence in Work Settings," *Academy
of Management Proceedings* 2021, no. 1 (August 2021): 12470,
https://doi.org/10.5465/ambpp.2021.12470.

7   **schools pushed for emotional literacy:** Parker Henry,
"Readin', Writin', and Regulatin' Emotions," *The New Yorker,*
June 20, 2022, https://www.newyorker.com/magazine
/2022/06/27/readin-writin-and-regulatin-emotions.

8   **"The limits of my language":** Ludwig Wittgenstein,
Tractatus Logico-Philosophicus, trans. C. K. Ogden (Dover
Publications, 1999), 88.

10   **whenever he was stuck:** Walter Isaacson, *Einstein: His Life and Universe* (Simon & Schuster, 2008).

PART 1 • Who You Are

13   **"Every now and then a man's mind":** Oliver Wendell Holmes, *The Autocrat of the Breakfast-Table* (Phillips, Sampson and Company, 1858): 311.

14   **Imagine being the chief financial officer:** Ravi Gupta, "Demanding and Supportive," *RKG.blog*, accessed April 16, 2025, https://www.rkg.blog/demanding.php.

CHAPTER 1 • The AQ Archetypes

17   **The privilege of a lifetime:** *Reflections on the Art of Living: A Joseph Campbell Companion*, ed. Diane K. Osbon (Harper Perennial, 1995), 15.

17   **where the temperatures climb:** "Sonoran Desert," in *Encyclopædia Britannica*, accessed February 28, 2025, https://www.britannica.com/place/Sonoran-Desert.

17   **Thousands of migrants:** Jason Motlagh, "The Deadliest Crossing," *Rolling Stone*, September 28, 2019, https://www.rollingstone.com/politics/politics-features/border-crisis-arizona-sonoran-desert-882613/.

25   **The Myers-Briggs Type Inventory says:** Sherrie Haynie, "Are Personalities Permanent? Can Your Personality Type Change?," Myers-Briggs Company, accessed April 16, 2025, https://www.themyersbriggs.com/en-US/Connect-With-Us/Blog/can-personality-type-change.

25   **the same is true for the Enneagram:** "How the Enneagram System Works," Enneagram Institute, February 28, 2024, https://www.enneagraminstitute.com/how-the-enneagram-system-works.

35   **Mae Jemison set off into space:** Matt Fratus, "The 1st African American Woman to Travel into Space Brought Along These Sentimental Items," *Coffee or Die*, February 18, 2021, https://www.coffeeordie.com/article/mae-jemison.

35   **In NASA's entire history, only 360:** NASA, *Astronaut Fact Book*, accessed December 18, 2024, https://www.nasa.gov /reference/astronaut-fact-book/.

35   **read through Jemison's biography:** Marisa Mathias, "Mae Jemison," National Women's History Museum, December 20, 2024, https://www.womenshistory.org /education-resources/biographies/mae-jemison.

36   **"Never be limited":** "Commencement Speaker: Dr. Mae Jemison," Berkeley School of Education, accessed April 16, 2025, https://bse.berkeley.edu/commencement-speaker-dr -mae-jemison.

CHAPTER 2 • Everything Changes

43   **"Nothing is absolute":** "Frida Kahlo Quotes," Frida Kahlo.org, accessed April 16, 2025, https://www.fridakahlo .org/frida-kahlo-quotes.jsp.

43   **In 1968, outside of Big Sur, California:** David Chadwick, *Crooked Cucumber: The Life and Teaching of Shunryu Suzuki* (Harmony/Rodale/Convergent, 2011): xi–xii.

45   **calls these experience "disruptors.":** Bruce Feiler, "Embracing the Nonlinear Life," in *Life Is in the Transitions: Mastering Change at Any Age* (Penguin Books, 2021), 52–73.

PART 2 • What You Think

67   **"All that we are is the result":** *The Dhammapada*, trans. Eknath Easwaran (Nilgiri Press, 2007), 105.

68   **they have names:** José Z. Abramson et al., "Imitation of

Novel Conspecific and Human Speech Sounds in the Killer Whale (*Orcinus orca*)," *Proceedings of the Royal Society B: Biological Sciences* 285, no. 1871 (January 31, 2018): 20172171, https://doi.org/10.1098/rspb.2017.2171.

68 **They form yearslong friendships:** Christa Lesté-Lasserre, "Killer Whales Form Killer Friendships, New Drone Footage Suggests," *Science,* June 17, 2021, https://www.science.org/content/article/killer-whales-form-killer-friendships-new-drone-footage-suggests.

68 **Keiko, who is better known as:** Susan Orlean, "Where's Willy?," *The New Yorker,* September 16, 2002, https://www.newyorker.com/magazine/2002/09/23/wheres-willy.

69 **"Rehabilitating a formerly captive whale":** Ferris Jabr, "Hvaldimir, the Whale Who Went AWOL," *The New York Times,* January 14, 2024, https://www.nytimes.com/2024/01/14/magazine/hvaldimir-whale.html.

69 **He played with toys:** Orlean, "Where's Willy?"

70 **During Keiko's rehabilitation:** Howard Garrett, "Keiko's Life Story," Orca Network, accessed April 16, 2025, https://www.orcanetwork.org/keiko-life-story.

70 **surrounded by grass that grew above:** Orlean, "Where's Willy?"

71 **On these sojourns, he'd follow:** Orlean, "Where's Willy?"

71 **He'd never hunted before:** Orlean, "Where's Willy?"

72 **He missed people:** Orlean, "Where's Willy?"

72 **Keiko's trainers stopped talking to him:** Nicole Barrantes, "The Story of Keiko, the First Captive Orca Returned to the Wild," World Animal Protection US, April 28, 2024, https://www.worldanimalprotection.us/latest/blogs/story-keiko-first-captive-orca-returned-wild/.

CHAPTER 3 • Anchors Aweigh

73 **"Be like the rocky headland":** Marcus Aurelius, *Meditations,* trans. Martin Hammond, ed. Diskin Clay (London: Penguin Classics, 2014), 33.

75 **Research on natural disasters shows:** National Academies of Sciences, Engineering, and Medicine, *Enhancing Community Resilience Through Social Capital and Connectedness: Stronger Together!* (The National Academies Press, 2021), https://doi.org/10.17226/26123.

75 **Elizabeth Duffy from Queens recalls:** Alyson Krueger, "10 Years Later, Hurricane Sandy Survivors Come to Ian Victims' Aid," *The New York Times,* October 12, 2022, https://www.nytimes.com/2022/10/12/nyregion /hurricane-sandy-ian.html.

81 **Maslow's hierarchy of needs:** A. H. Maslow, "A Theory of Human Motivation," *Psychological Review* 50, no. 4 (1943): 370–96, https://doi.org/10.1037/h0054346.

81 **Countless studies confirm:** Müge Simsek et al., "Childhood Residential Mobility and Health Outcomes: A Meta-Analysis," *Health & Place* 71 (September 2021): 102650, https://doi.org/10.1016/j.healthplace.2021.102650.

82 **Jonathan Slon's apartment:** D. W. Gibson, "The New York Apartment That Has Sheltered One Family for 86 Years," *The New York Times,* September 9, 2024, https://www .nytimes.com/2024/09/09/realestate/renters-manhattan -morningside-heights.html.

83 **24,020 rent-controlled units:** "Rent Control FAQs," Rent Guidelines Board, accessed April 16, 2025, https:// rentguidelinesboard.cityofnewyork.us/resources/faqs/rent -control/.

83 **almost 4 million apartments:** "Fast Facts About NYC

Housing," Tenant Protection Cabinet, NYC.gov, accessed April 16, 2025, https://www.nyc.gov/content/tenant protection/pages/fast-facts-about-housing-in-nyc.

83   **He and the rest of his kin:** Gibson, "The New York Apartment."

83   **it's connected more than sixteen thousand people:** The Dinner Party Labs, *2023 Impact Report*, n.d., https://drive .google.com/file/d/13PyYzjv176xAZrViPhcIbA_UJgtB IeOF/view.

CHAPTER 4 • Wanna Bet?

87   **"Sometimes your only available transportation":** Quoted in Kay Wills Wyma, *I'm Happy for You (Sort Of . . . Not Really): Finding Contentment in a Culture of Comparison* (PRH Christian Publishing, 2015), 34.

88   **Ambiguity Aversion is a psychological bias:** Daniel Ellsberg, "Risk, Ambiguity, and the Savage Axioms," *The Quarterly Journal of Economics* 75, no. 4 (November 1961): 643–69, https://doi.org/10.2307/1884324.

89   **Ambiguity Aversion has deep evolutionary roots:** Kristen Hawkes et al., "The Behavioral Ecology of Modern Hunter-Gatherers, and Human Evolution," *Trends in Ecology & Evolution* 12, no. 1 (January 1997): 29–32, https://doi .org/10.1016/s0169-5347(96)10060-4.

93   **In finance, hedging:** Thomas J. Catalano, "Beginner's Guide to Hedging: Definition and Example of Hedges in Finance," *Investopedia,* June 16, 2024, https://www .investopedia.com/trading/hedging-beginners-guide.

94   **As Newton's first law of motion:** "Newton's Laws of Motion," in *Encyclopædia Britannica,* accessed April 17, 2025, https://www.britannica.com/science/Newtons-laws-of -motion.

96   **Tyler Perry made thirteen bets:** "Tyler Perry's Story,"
      Tyler Perry, accessed April 17, 2025, https://tylerperry.com
      /tyler/story/.

96   **Brian Acton made and lost:** Nicole Nguyen, "The
      Founders of WhatsApp Prove Perseverance Wins," PopSugar,
      February 20, 2014, https://www.popsugar.com/tech
      /whatsapp-founders-jan-koum-brian-acton-34113022.

96   **It took him nine hundred bets:** "10 Things You Might
      Not Know About Vincent van Gogh," Google Arts &
      Culture, accessed April 17, 2025, https://artsandculture
      .google.com/story/10-things-you-might-not-know-about
      -vincent-van-gogh/AgXRtrYjblBRKA?hl=en.

96   **to get his first real sale:** Brian Boucher, "The Story of the
      Only Known Painting Van Gogh Sold During His Lifetime,"
      Artnet News, February 12, 2024, https://news.artnet.com/art
      -world/story-only-known-painting-van-gogh-sold-2432275.

CHAPTER 5 • Class Is in Session

103   **"A whole lifetime is needed":** Seneca, *How to Die: An
      Ancient Guide to the End of Life,* ed. and trans. James S. Romm
      (Princeton University Press, 2018), xx.

103   **"Nothing ever goes away":** Pema Chödrön, *When Things
      Fall Apart: Heart Advice for Difficult Times* (Shambhala, 2000), 85.

105   **When Satya Nadella took over:** Stephen McBride, "The
      Secret Trait of Stocks That Soar 1,000%+," Yahoo! Finance,
      March 1, 2020, https://finance.yahoo.com/news/secret-trait
      -stocks-soar.

105   **Some investors put pressure on Microsoft:** Tara
      Lachapelle and Brooke Sutherland, "Less Microsoft Is More as
      Investors Eye Breakup: Real M&A," *Bloomberg,* February 4,
      2014, https://www.bloomberg.com/news/articles/2014-02
      -04/less-microsoft-is-more-as-investors-eye-breakup-real-m-a.

106   **While there were sweeping strategic decisions:** Harry
        McCracken, "Transforming Culture at Microsoft: Satya
        Nadella Sets a New Tone," *INTHEBLACK*, June 1, 2018,
        https://intheblack.cpaaustralia.com.au/people/satya-nadella
        -transforming-culture-microsoft.

106   **by teaching Microsoft the agility tool:** Paul Argenti et al.,
        "The Secret Behind Successful Corporate Transformations,"
        Harvard Business Review, September 14, 2021, https://hbr
        .org/2021/09/the-secret-behind-successful-corporate
        -transformations.

106   **He and his team created:** Argenti et al., "The Secret
        Behind Successful Corporate Transformations."

106   **Nadella pushed new processes:** "How Satya Nadella Led
        Microsoft Through a Corporate Turnaround," NOBL
        Collective, July 12, 2024, https://nobl.io/changemaker/how
        -satya-nadella-led-microsoft-through-a-corporate-turnaround.

110   **Nelson Mandela was a Nobel Peace Prize winner:**
        "Nelson Mandela," in *Encyclopædia Britannica,* accessed April 10,
        2025, https://www.britannica.com/biography/Nelson
        -Mandela.

110   **he made it his goal to listen:** Richard Stengel, "Mandela:
        His 8 Lessons of Leadership," *Time,* July 9, 2008, https://time
        .com/archive/6685457/mandela-his-8-lessons-of-leadership/.

110   **A Harvard Business School study:** A. W. Brooks et al.,
        "Smart People Ask for (My) Advice: Seeking Advice Boosts
        Perceptions of Competence," *Management Science* 61, no. 6
        (June 2015): 1421–35.

112   **At age twenty-four, Agassi beat:** Andre Agassi, *Open: An
        Autobiography* (Vintage, 2010).

112   **"I'm the number one tennis player":** Agassi, *Open,* 204.

112   **Agassi started using crystal meth:** "Andre Agassi's
        Extraordinary Journey," CBS News, November 5, 2009,

https://www.cbsnews.com/news/andre-agassis-extraordinary
-journey/.

112   **In 2003, at age thirty-three:** McCarton Ackerman, "Andre
Agassi: From Rebel to Philosopher," ATP Tour, July 9, 2020,
https://www.atptour.com/en/news/agassi-number-one
-profile.

116   **Sister Madonna Buder completed:** Margie Zable Fisher,
"At 92 Years Young, the 'Iron Nun' Is Still Running,"
Triathlete, September 29, 2021, https://www.triathlete.com
/culture/people/at-91-years-young-the-iron-nun-is-still
-running/.

116   **Yuichiro Miura climbed Mount Everest:** Bill Chappell,
" 'On Top of the World' at 80: Japanese Climber Summits
Everest," NPR, May 23, 2013, https://www.npr.org/sections
/thetwo-way/2013/05/23/186240274/on-top-of-the-world
-at-80-japanese-climber-summits-everest.

CHAPTER 6 • The Discomfort Wave

118   **"Barn's burnt down":** In David Schiller, *The Little Zen
Companion* (Workman Publishing, 1994), 147.

118   **The physical experience of childbirth rates:** R. Melzack,
"The Myth of Painless Childbirth (the John J. Bonica Lecture),"
Pain 19, no. 4 (August 1984): 321–37, https://doi.org/10
.1016/0304-3959(84)90079-4.

121   **In 1951, a Canadian psychologist:** Michael Mechanic,
"What Extreme Isolation Does to Your Mind," *Mother Jones*,
October 18, 2012, https://www.motherjones.com/politics
/2012/10/donald-o-hebb-effects-extreme-isolation/.

128   **"Nothing beautiful in the end comes":** The Dalai Lama
and Desmond Tutu, with Douglas Abrams, *The Book of Joy:
Lasting Happiness in a Changing World* (Avery, 2016), 45.

SUMMARY OF PART 2 • Your CHURN, Your Choice

130   **if you walked into the back rooms:** Pete Wells, "After 12 Years of Reviewing Restaurants, I'm Leaving the Table," *The New York Times,* July 16, 2024, https://www.nytimes.com /2024/07/16/dining/pete-wells-steps-down-food-critic.html.

130   **a coveted job that required him:** Tim Carman, "*New York Times* Food Critic Pete Wells Steps Down, Citing His Health," *The Washington Post,* July 16, 2024, https://www.washington post.com/food/2024/07/16/pete-wells-new-york-times -restaurant-critic/.

131   **"We avoid mentioning weight":** Wells, "I'm Leaving the Table."

131   **a visit to his doctor revealed:** Wells, "I'm Leaving the Table."

132   **It all started with a fire extinguisher:** Sean Cole and Sarah Polley, "Swim Towards the Shark," *This American Life,* NPR, August 9, 2024, https://www.thisamericanlife.org/837 /swim-towards-the-shark.

134   **Drew Bouton, a policy director:** Bonnie Rochman, "For 22 Years, Drew Bouton Has Lived with Metastatic Prostate Cancer," Fred Hutch Cancer Center, January 15, 2024, https://www.fredhutch.org/en/news/center-news/2024 /01/22-years-with-metastatic-prostate-cancer.html.

PART 3 • What You Do

139   **"A man grows most tired":** Quoted in Kate Eckman, *The Full Spirit Workout: A Ten-Step System to Shed Your Self-Doubt, Strengthen Your Spiritual Core, and Create a Fun and Fulfilling Life* (New World Library, 2021), 13.

140   **Thought leaders and scientists:** "Report of the

Commission: The Influence of Railway Travelling on Public Health," *The Lancet* 1 (January 25, 1862): 107–10.

141 **"The only thing we know":** Peter F. Drucker, *Management: Tasks, Responsibilities, Practices* (Harper & Row, 1974), 44.

CHAPTER 7 • Get Durable

143 **"Man is still the most extraordinary":** John F. Kennedy, "Remarks upon Presenting the NASA Distinguished Service Medal to Astronaut L. Gordon Cooper," May 21, 1963, The American Presidency Project, https://www.presidency.ucsb .edu/documents/remarks-upon-presenting-the-nasa -distinguished-service-medal-astronaut-l-gordon-cooper.

144 **This question of monkey or pedestal:** Astro Teller, "Tackle the Monkey First," *Medium,* December 7, 2016, https://blog.x.company/tackle-the-monkey-first-90fd6223 e04d.

144 **monitoring ocean health:** Astro Teller, "Tidal's Next Wave," *Google X Blog,* July 12, 2024, https://x.company/blog /posts/tidalgraduation/.

144 **beaming the internet through lasers:** "Taara—a Google X Moonshot," X, accessed April 17, 2025, https://x.company /projects/taara/.

144 **creating grid-scale energy storage:** The Team at X, "Introducing Malta," *Medium,* December 19, 2018, https:// blog.x.company/introducing-malta-81bceb559061.

145 **Since the mid-1900s:** "The Invention of the Career Ladder," BBC News, July 24, 2013, https://www.bbc.com /news/magazine-23419229.

146 **According to Harvard's:** Jorge Tamayo et al., "Reskilling in the Age of AI," *Harvard Business Review,* September 1, 2023, hbr .org/2023/09/reskilling-in-the-age-of-ai.

147 **In 1902, two brothers:** "Hermès," *Acquired* (podcast), season 14, episode 2, February 19, 2024, https://www .acquired.fm/episodes/hermes.

148 **one of the highest-valued luxury brands:** Reuters, "Hermès Overtakes LVMH to Become the World's Most Valuable Luxury Company," CNN, April 15, 2025, https:// www.cnn.com/2025/04/15/style/hermes-worlds-most -valuable-luxury-company.

148 **When Émile-Maurice visited the Ford factories:** "Hermès," *Acquired.*

CHAPTER 8 • The High-AQ Team

159 **"A single arrow is easily broken":** Daniel Crump Buchanan, *Japanese Proverbs and Sayings* (University of Oklahoma Press, 1965), 113.

CHAPTER 9 • The High-AQ Manager

165 **"In the universe":** Lao Tsu, *Tao Te Ching,* trans. Gia-Fu Feng and Jane English (Vintage Books, 1989), 66.

165 **Before Nike was Nike:** Phil Knight, *Shoe Dog: A Memoir by the Creator of Nike* (Simon & Schuster, 2018), 207–8.

CHAPTER 10 • Green & Black Thinking

173 **"The test of a first-rate intelligence":** "Essay: The Crack-Up by F. Scott Fitzgerald," PBS, November 3, 2022, https://www.pbs.org/wnet/americanmasters/f-scott -fitzgerald-essay-the-crack-up/1028/.

174 **In 1985, a cognitive theorist:** Edward de Bono, *Six Thinking Hats* (Penguin, 2009).

180 **Starting with the black hat:** "Nvidia Part I: The GPU

Company (1993–2006)," *Acquired* (podcast), season 10, episode 5, March 27, 2022, https://www.acquired.fm /episodes/nvidia-the-gpu-company-1993-2006.

181 **NVIDIA is worth more than $3 trillion:** "Nvidia Surpasses Apple as World's Biggest Company, Valued at $3.43 Trillion," *The Economic Times*, November 6, 2024, https:// economictimes.indiatimes.com/tech/technology/nvidia -surpasses-apple-as-worlds-biggest-company.

181 **When Jensen was growing up:** "Nvidia Part I," *Acquired.*

181 **the Huangs lacked the finances:** Brian Dumaine, "The Man Who Came Back from the Dead Again and Again," CNNMoney, September 1, 2001, https://money.cnn.com /magazines/fsb/fsb_archive/2001/09/01/309500/index .htm.

182 **He and his roommate, who was:** Dumaine, "The Man Who Came Back from the Dead."

182 **In 2019, with gratitude:** "Former Student's Gift Paves the Way for New Facility," Oneida Baptist Institute, accessed April 17, 2025, https://www.oneidaschool.org/about/huang hall.cfm.

183 **He was the world's oldest:** Sam Roberts, "Irving Kahn, Oldest Active Wall Street Investor, Dies at 109," *The New York Times*, February 26, 2015, https://www.nytimes.com/2015 /02/27/business/irving-kahn-oldest-active-wall-street-investor -dies-at-109.html.

183 **he advocated for greater accountability:** Roberts, "Irving Kahn."

183 **Today, hundreds of thousands of people:** Lananh Nguyen, "Only 35% Pass Wall St.'s Toughest Test. How Much Does That Matter?," *The New York Times*, September 30, 2021, https://www.nytimes.com/2021/09/30/business/cfa-test-fail -pass.html.

183 **When he was seventy-three, he founded:** Laurence
Arnold, "Irving Kahn, Investor Who Profited in '29 Crash,
Dies at 109," *Bloomberg*, February 26, 2015, https://www
.bloomberg.com/news/articles/2015-02-26/irving-kahn
-investor-who-made-money-in-1929-crash-dies-at-109.

184 **broadened to a Kindle e-reader:** Taryn Winter Brill and
Irving Kahn, "World's Oldest Stockbroker Trading Strong at
105," CBS News, December 14, 2011.

184 **He scrutinized every piece:** "The Life of Kahn: 109 Years
of Wisdom," *Investment Values* 115 (July 2015), https://cheviot
.com/articles/the-life-of-kahn-109-years-of-wisdom/.

CHAPTER 11 • Bushwhack Like a Camel

187 **"Life shrinks or expands":** "Anaïs Nin," Oxford Reference,
https://www.oxfordreference.com/display/10.1093/acref
/9780191843730.001.0001/q-oro-ed5-00007902, accessed
May 23, 2025.

187 **Camels walked a long way:** Peter D. Heintzman et al.,
"Genomic Data from Extinct North American *Camelops* Revise
Camel Evolutionary History," *Molecular Biology and Evolution* 32,
no. 9 (June 2, 2015): 2433–40, https://doi.org/10.1093/mol
bev/msv128.

188 **It turns out these features:** Jo Price, "How Did the Camel
Get Its Hump?," *Discover Wildlife*, January 6, 2025, https://
www.discoverwildlife.com/animal-facts/mammals/how-did
-the-camel-get-its-hump.

188 **Some species, like the Adélie:** Bill Weir, *Life as We Know It
(Can Be): Stories of People, Climate, and Hope in a Changing World*
(Chronicle Prism, 2024).

188 **Others, like the Gentoo penguin:** Elizabeth Claire Alberts,
"As Climate Change Melts Antarctic Ice, Gentoo Penguins
Venture Further South," Mongabay, January 21, 2022,

https://news.mongabay.com/2022/01/as-climate-change
-melts-antarctic-ice-gentoo-penguins-venture-further-south/.

188 **rigid penguins, stuck in the past:** "Penguins and Climate
Change," British Antarctic Survey, July 4, 2022, https://www
.bas.ac.uk/data/our-data/publication/penguins/.

189 **She was the daughter:** "Maggie Lena Draper Walker," in
Encyclopædia Britannica, accessed April 17, 2025, https://www
.britannica.com/money/Maggie-Lena-Draper-Walker.

190 **it was a crime:** Candice Frederick, "'Loving' and the History
of Anti-Miscegenation Laws in Virginia and Washington,"
New York Public Library, Schomburg Center for Research in
Black Culture, https://www.nypl.org/blog/2016/11/03
/loving-and-history.

190 **At the age of eleven:** Kathryn S. Gardiner, "Forgotten
Foremothers: Maggie Lena Walker," League of Women Voters
of Muncie-Delaware County, March 10, 2023, https://
lwvmunciedelaware.org/content.aspx?page_id=5&club
_id=468470&item_id=86087.

190 **Free Black women in Virginia:** Jonathan Grossman,
"Black Studies in the Department of Labor 1897–1907," U.S.
Department of Labor, accessed April 17, 2025, https://www
.dol.gov/general/aboutdol/history/blackstudiestext.

190 **by law, she'd have to leave:** Elena Botella, "Banking on
Black Women: Inside Maggie Walker's Financial Empire,"
Scalawag, June 17, 2019, https://scalawagmagazine.org
/2019/06/virginia-black-banking/.

191 **He learned to catch his own fish:** Susan Orlean, "Where's
Willy?," *The New Yorker,* September 16, 2002, https://www.new
yorker.com/magazine/2002/09/23/wheres-willy.

191 **At sixteen, while still in school:** "Lessons from Maggie
Lena Walker's Entrepreneurial Leadership," *HBR on Leadership,*
episode 70, August 7, 2024.

193 **In 1899, when Maggie Lena Walker:** John Mullin, "Maggie Lena Walker," Federal Reserve Bank of Richmond, accessed April 17, 2025, https://www.richmondfed.org /publications/research/econ_focus/2022/q4_economic _history.

194 **First, Maggie led a massive recruiting drive:** "Lessons from Maggie Lena Walker's Entrepreneurial Leadership," *HBR on Leadership*.

194 **she built personal relationships:** "Lessons from Maggie Lena Walker's Entrepreneurial Leadership," *HBR on Leadership*.

194 **the order's membership grew to seventy thousand:** Botella, "Banking on Black Women."

194 **they expanded their insurance fund:** National Museum of African American History & Culture, "Independent Order of St. Luke," Searchable Museum, accessed April 17, 2025, https://www.searchablemuseum.com/independent-order-of -st-luke.

195 **in 1905, the order opened an emporium:** "Maggie Lena Walker (1864–1934)," in *Encyclopedia Virginia*, accessed February 18, 2025, https://encyclopediavirginia.org/entries/walker -maggie-lena-1864-1934.

SUMMARY OF PART 3 • The Great Equalizer

201 **employees with high learning agility:** Guangrong Dai et al., "The Role of Learning Agility in Executive Career Success: The Results of Two Field Studies," *Journal of Managerial Issues* 25, no. 2 (July 2013): 108–31.

201 **a study by Christopher Lee Bedford:** Christopher Lee Bedford, "The Role of Learning Agility in Workplace Performance and Career Advancement" (PhD diss., University of Minnesota, June 2011), https://conservancy.umn.edu

/server/api/core/bitstreams/f6ced063-db50-45d2-9c0a
-c9f557f094c6/content.

CONCLUSION • The Full AQ Life

203 **"To improve is to change":** Quoted in Dominique Enright, *The Wicked Wit of Winston Churchill* (ReadHowYouWant, 2015), 25.

204 **a child's brain is 90 percent fully grown:** "Learning Begins at Birth," The Children's Reading Foundation, https://www.readingfoundation.org/learning-begins-at-birth.

204 **by age ten they've learned twenty thousand words:** ACT, "Cognitive and Social Skills to Expect from 6 to 10 Years," American Psychological Association, accessed April 17, 2025, https://www.apa.org/act/resources/fact-sheets/development-10-years.

204 **"In youth we may have":** William James, *The Principles of Psychology* Vols. 1-2 (Pantianos Classics, 2017), 261.

Index

ABOUT THE AUTHOR

LIZ TRAN is the founder of Inner Genius and a leadership coach to CEOs and founders of some of the world's fastest-growing companies. She is also the author of *The Karma of Success,* and her work has been featured by *Today, The New Yorker, The New York Times,* Bloomberg, *Fast Company, Entrepreneur,* and other outlets. She lives with her husband and daughters in New York City and Norfolk, Connecticut.